CULTURES OF THE WORLD

SCOTLAND

Patricia Levy

MARSHALL CAVENDISH
New York • London • Sydney

Reference edition reprinted 2001 by
Marshall Cavendish Corporation
99 White Plains Road
Tarrytown
New York 10591

© Times Media Private Limited 2000

Originated and designed by
Times Books International, an imprint of
Times Media Private Limited, a member of the
Times Publishing Group

Printed in Malaysia

Library of Congress Cataloging-in-Publication Data:

Levy, Patricia, 1951 –
    Scotland / Patricia Levy.
        p. cm.—(Cultures of the World)
    Includes bibliographical references (p.) and index.
    ISBN 0-7614-1159-3
    1. Scotland—Juvenile literature. [1. Scotland.] I. Title.
II. Series.

DA762.L58 2001
941.1—dc21   00–039831
                CIP
                AC

INTRODUCTION

After being a part of the United Kingdom for nearly three centuries, Scotland has recently voted to have its own regional parliament. Its climate and much of its culture set it apart from its southern neighbors. Its geography is one of remote Highlands, vast lochs, towering mountains, and busy cities. Its history is one of invasions, rebellions, Highland clearances, and in more modern times, a struggle for a sense of identity within Europe. Plants and animals that are rare in the rest of Britain survive here, while on the remote islands, Gaelic, the ancient language of Scotland, is still spoken.

This book, part of the Cultures of the World series, looks at Scotland and the Scots. It offers a glimpse of a country that has for many years been overshadowed by its more populous and economically stronger neighbor, England. It also provides insights into a country that is more than just haggis, bagpipes, and the Loch Ness monster.

CONTENTS

A female piper takes a breather during a bagpipe performance.

CONTENTS

A performer at the annual Fringe Festival in Edinburgh, which is held in August.

GEOGRAPHY

SCOTLAND MAKES UP about one-third of the island of Britain. It is bordered by England in the south, the Atlantic Ocean along its western and northern coasts, and the North Sea on the east. The mainland of Scotland consists of an area of 28,269 square miles (73,217 square km), while the islands surrounding it have a total area of 2,149 square miles (5,566 square km).

Scotland's mainland stretches 274 miles (441 km) from Cape Wrath in the north to the Mull of Galloway in the south, and 154 miles (284 km) from Applecross in the western Highlands to Buchan Ness in the eastern Grampians. Scotland's coastline is deeply indented by a series of fjords, and very few places are more than 50 miles (80 km) from the coast. The distance between the Firth of Clyde and Firth of Forth, which are estuaries in the west and east, is only 30 miles (48 km).

Scotland is a hilly country and can be divided into three geographic regions—the Highlands, Central Lowlands, and Southern Uplands. The Highlands make up two-thirds of northern Scotland and include the highest mountain, Ben Nevis, at 4,406 feet (1,343 m). The Highlands are divided by the Great Glen, a geological fault line. Located in the Glen are a number of lochs, or lakes, of which Loch Ness is the largest.

The Central Lowlands consist of a triangular area that is made up of Glasgow in the west and Dundee and Edinburgh in the east. The numerous towns that are home to most of Scotland's population and bulk of its industry are located here.

The Southern Uplands is a hilly region, with elevations no higher than 1,500 feet (457 m). Scotland's highest village, Wanlockhead, at 1,380 feet (421 m), can be found here.

Above: **A nesting colony of gannets on Unst Island, Scotland's most northerly island.**

Opposite: **The 160-feet-(48-m) high Old Man of Storr, found on the Isle of Skye. This rock pinnacle is surrounded by black cliffs and overlooks the Storr Lochs.**

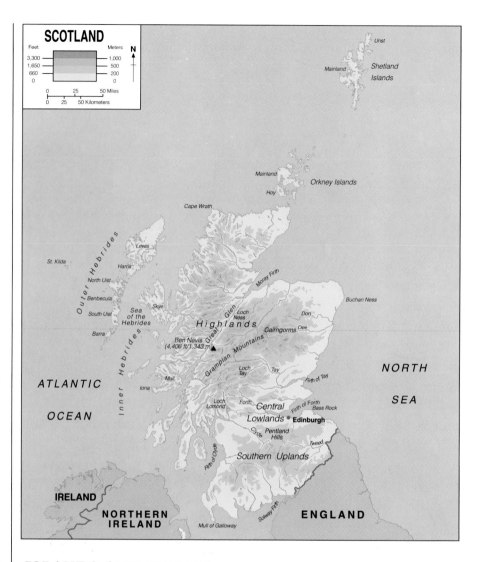

SCOTLAND

Feet		Meters
3,300		1,000
1,650		500
660		200
0		0

N

0   25   50 Miles
0   25   50 Kilometers

Unst

Shetland
Islands

Mainland

Mainland

Orkney Islands

Hoy

Cape Wrath

Lewis

St. Kilda

Harris

North Uist

Moray Firth

Benbecula

Skye

Buchan Ness

South Uist

Sea
of the
Hebrides

Loch
Ness

Don

Barra

Highlands

Cairngorms

Dee

Ben Nevis
(4,406 ft/1,343 m)

Grampian Mountains

NORTH

Mull

Loch
Tay

Tay

Firth of Tay

Iona

SEA

ATLANTIC

Loch
Lomond

Forth

Central
Lowlands

Firth of Forth

Bass Rock

OCEAN

Edinburgh

Clyde

Pentland
Hills

Tweed

Firth of Clyde

Southern Uplands

IRELAND

Solway Firth

ENGLAND

**NORTHERN
IRELAND**

Mull of Galloway

Opposite: **The exterior**
(left) **and interior of** *(right)*
Fingal's Cave, on Staffa
Island, which is 6 miles
(10 km) north of Iona Is-
land.

ISLANDS AND RIVERS

Scotland has 790 islands, most of which are part of the Hebrides to the west and the Orkney and Shetland island groups to the north. Only 62 islands exceed 3 square miles (8 square km). Of the 26 rivers flowing directly into the sea, the most significant are the Clyde and Tweed Rivers that originate in the Southern Uplands and the Forth and Tay Rivers that flow from the Highlands. The Clyde, Forth, and Tay Rivers open into large estuaries and support respectively the cities of Glasgow, Edinburgh, and Dundee.

HOW SCOTLAND ARRIVED WHERE IT IS TODAY

About 2,500 million years ago, the land mass that is now Scotland was detached from the rest of what is now Britain. It was located somewhere south of the equator. Some time later the tectonic plate it is attached to began to move north. About 500 million years ago the ocean basin that divided Scotland from England and Wales rose. The thrusting and folding motion of the earth's crust created the Scottish Highlands.

Four hundred million years ago the European and American tectonic plates collided. For some time Scotland was attached to North America. Great rivers washed down sand from the north and created the sandstone rocks now found on Hoy Island.

About 370 million years ago Britain had moved north as far as the equator. Parts of Scotland lay in a warm shallow sea, and a salt-tolerant vegetation developed. Some of these trees can still be seen in the Fossil Grove, in the middle of Glasgow, but only the fossilized stumps of the trees remain. These trees were probably 100 feet (30 m) high, with regular, symmetrical roots and a tough outer bark.

As the British isles gradually floated northward, dinosaurs roamed the Highlands of Scotland. Around 60 million years ago America started to head westward, and the Atlantic Ocean formed. The resulting volcanic activity threw up Scotland's newest mountains, the Western Highlands. At the same time strange volcanic rock formations such as Fingal's Cave, the hexagonal rock on Staffa Island, were created.

About 2.5 million years ago the Ice Age hit Scotland. The western side of the country shows signs of the great glaciers that formed deep U-shaped valleys. As the ice melted, the land rose and raised beaches developed. The last Ice Age created the landscape of today's Scotland.

The snow-capped Ben Lawers (3,982 feet/ 1,214 m), Scotland's ninth tallest mountain, towers above Loch Tay.

CLIMATE

Scotland has a varied climate. Its geographic position in northern Europe gives it a temperate climate, while the presence of the Gulf Stream along the western coastline gives some parts a warm climate even in winter. The Highlands of Scotland, especially the Cairngorm plateau, are the highest in Britain, and this area rarely loses its snow cover, even in the summer. The Highlands often experience high winds and cloud cover. Ben Nevis, for example, is exposed to gales that travel at 50 miles per hour (80 km per hour) for as much as two-thirds of the year.

In the far north, for much of the summer, daytime can last for as long as 20 hours. The east coast has the most hours of sunshine and is less affected by the prevailing westerly winds. In the spring and winter there are often dry easterly winds that bring cold continental air masses to the country. Rainfall is variable, with the Highlands receiving up to 140 inches (3,560 mm) of rain per year, while the east coast gets as little as 25 inches (640 mm) of rain in some years.

FLORA

Plant life that has disappeared in the rest of Britain because of urbanization and changing agricultural patterns can be found in Scotland. Its mild westerly climate supports delicate plants, while the Highlands are home to creatures more commonly seen in the Arctic. One endangered habitat still common in the Scottish mountains is the raised bog, where great domes of sphagnum moss build up and then die, creating islands of dry land in upland lakes. On these domes a multitude of rare and endangered bog species, such as the carnivorous sundew, thrive.

Scotland also has some oak woodlands, but the most common tree is the conifer, which is cultivated as a cash crop. These quick-growing trees are deliberately planted close together so that they grow tall. At ground level, rare plants such as wintergreen (which is used to make medicine), twinflower (a tiny pink flower with two flower heads), wood anemones, and bluebells or wild hyacinth can be found. The national emblem of Scotland is the thistle, a prickly plant with purple flowers.

Bog cotton on the Isle of Skye.

Above: **Golden eagles were poisoned by game-keepers who wanted to protect game birds, which were shot for sport.**

Opposite: **Underneath the placid, furry appearance of Highland cattle lies a ferocious nature.**

FAUNA

In the 12th century reindeer roamed freely in the valleys of Scotland. They were, however, later hunted to extinction. Recently herds of reindeer have been reintroduced on the slopes of the Cairngorms. Also living in the mountains are red deer. Around a quarter of a million red deer survive despite culling, hunting, and the harsh winters. The most magnificent bird to be found in the Scottish mountains is the once endangered golden eagle. It now breeds happily in the Highlands. Named after its golden nape feathers, the golden eagle has a wing span of 8 feet (2.1 m) and hunts young sheep and other small mammals.

Scotland's natural woodlands are home to many unusual creatures such as the black grouse and capercaillie, large game-birds that used to be hunted. Another inhabitant of the woodlands is the Scots crossbill, whose only habitat is the Scottish pine forests.

Scotland has a long coastline and many offshore islands, which are resting places for migrant birds from the Arctic. These islands, many of them no bigger than a rock, also support colonies of Manx shearwater, great skuas (one-third of the entire northern hemisphere population), and hundreds of thousands of common seabirds. Scotland has one-half of the world's population of Atlantic seals breeding around its shores, but in recent years they have been threatened by the increase in fish farms. Many are either poisoned by the chemicals used to prevent fish diseases or shot by fish farmers wishing to protect their stock.

SWONA CATTLE

Highland cattle are a very distinctive breed of cattle that can survive in extreme conditions for long periods. They are semiwild creatures, with large horns and long, reddish brown hair.

One particular group of Highland cattle found on Swona Island, part of the Orkney Islands, has evolved into a new species called Swona cattle. Their ancestors were abandoned by human population about 30 years ago to breed and fend for themselves.

Swona cattle are aggressive toward humans and breed only once a year, unlike domestic cows, which are artificially bred to produce milk all year. They have also evolved a social system of their own, which domestic animals never have since they are separated from the herd at birth and few domestic bulls are allowed to grow to adulthood. On Swona Island the bulls have developed naturally, and the herd has about five males that dominate the herd—the other bulls have been driven out and live in isolation.

A view of Princes Street in Edinburgh.

CITIES

The four major cities in Scotland are Edinburgh, Glasgow, Aberdeen, and Dundee. All are located on the banks of Scotland's main rivers or estuaries.

EDINBURGH is the capital of Scotland and is situated in east-central Scotland between the Pentland Hills and the southern shores of the Firth of Forth. The population is around 500,000. Clerical and service-oriented industries predominate, and the city is also a center for the legal profession. Recently Edinburgh has become the political center of Scotland, with large numbers of government employees and members of the Scottish Parliament based in the city.

Edinburgh is home to the new Scottish Parliament and serves as the headquarters for most of the Scottish banks and the brewing and distilling industries. It is a center for publishing and has two universities, Herriot Watt and Edinburgh. Edinburgh's other major industry is tourism. Thousands of visitors flock to the city in the summer, especially during the Edinburgh International Festival.

GLASGOW is derived from the Celtic *Glas Ghu*, meaning "Green Glen." The city, with a population of about 800,000, is Scotland's largest and most densely populated city. It is located along both banks of the Clyde River, 20 miles (32 km) from the mouth of the river. The city and its suburbs occupy most of the surrounding valley. The city has a large commercial and administrative area located north of the river. The river itself is lined with shipyards and engineering businesses, although far fewer than once existed. Other industries are whisky blending and bottling, and the manufacture of chemicals, textiles, and carpets.

Glasgow was once famous for its slum areas, especially an area called the Gorbals, but now most of the shantytowns have been cleared. The city is expanding all the time so that towns that were once quite independent of the city, such as East Kilbride, Cumbernauld, Glenrothes, and Livingstone, have now become city suburbs. This has helped to reduce inner-city congestion.

Glasgow has shaken off the image of an industrial center and has recently received awards for design and architecture. It has an airport, railroads, and a public transportation system. Glasgow also boasts of a university that is five centuries old.

Buchanan Street in Glasgow is the heart of the shopping district.

ABERDEEN, which lies between the Don and Dee Rivers, is Scotland's third largest city with a population of around 210,000. It is the center of the North Sea energy industry and is known as the "oil capital of Europe." Aberdeen's extensive harbor is home to fishing and energy supply boats, and its chief industry is servicing the North Sea oil rigs. A smaller industry is the production and shipping of granite.

DUNDEE is Scotland's fourth largest city. Situated on the east coast of Scotland on the banks of the Tay River, it has a population of more than 200,000. Like Aberdeen, Dundee has been influenced by the development of North Sea oil. Other industries include shipbuilding, and the manufacturing of jute, textiles, paper, confectionery, and electronic appliances. A major employer is D.C. Thomson, which publishes the popular comics *Beano* and *Dandy*, as well as one of Scotland's national daily papers.

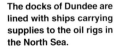

The docks of Dundee are lined with ships carrying supplies to the oil rigs in the North Sea.

NATURAL RESOURCES

Coal was once Scotland's main natural resource and a leading factor in the industrialization of the country. Most of the accessible coal resources are now defunct. In 1913 peak production stood at 42.3 million tons (43 million metric tons) per year. In recent years only a few opencast mines were still in operation. Other natural resources that have been mined commercially at various times include gold, silver, dolomite, granite, and chromite. These are, however, not mined in large enough quantities today to maintain the industries. Peat is another valuable resource and is used domestically for fuel in the Highlands. It is not mined commercially as a lot of time and effort is required to cut and dry the peat.

A farmer using a special tool called the peat-iron to cut peat. Compared to wood or coal, peat takes a longer time to burn and produces a characteristic odor.

North Sea oil has had an enormous effect on the economic geography of Scotland, developing the towns and service industries nearest the oil fields. Most of the revenue from the sale of oil goes to the government in Britain and is not available to the government of Scotland. As production from the oil fields has slowed, North Sea gas has begun to replace it as an energy source.

Scotland has vast areas of water in its sea lochs and inland waters, which has provided another resource—electricity. There are several hydroelectric power stations in Scotland using pumped storage schemes. In these schemes, electricity is used in off-peak hours to pump water to a high dam. The water is then released at times of peak electricity usage and operates turbogenerators. Other means of generating electricity include nuclear power stations at Torness, east of Edinburgh, and Dounreay, in the Highlands. There are a few oil-fired power stations.

HISTORY

THE FIRST EVIDENCE of human habitation in Scotland has been found on the raised beaches and dates from the third millennium B.C. These early inhabitants from England, Ireland, and northern Europe were hunter-gatherers. Around the second millennium B.C., the inhabitants started to farm and raise livestock. Later they progressed to a point where they could build huge chamber tombs such as those at Maes Howe in the Orkney Islands or sophisticated stone houses such as those discovered at Skara Brae, also in the Orkneys. The civilizations that built these grand tombs, houses, and standing stone alignments lived on the western and northern islands of Scotland. Although these places are now barren agriculturally (being largely peat bog), the land was much more fertile during Neolithic times when the climate in northern Scotland was mild and less wet.

Between 2000 and 1500 B.C. a Bronze Age culture was introduced to Scotland by the Beaker People from mainland Europe, so named for the shape of their drinking vessels. These people understood the process of bronze making and created metal weapons and tools that made land clearance and farming easier. Remains of Bronze Age Scotland can be found at Callanish on Lewis Island and Brodgar in the Orkney Islands.

The Iron Age developed in Scotland around 500 B.C. by the Celts from Europe. They brought with them iron tools. Many of them lived in ring forts, banked earthen compounds with mud and wattle houses and often an underground passage for escape or storage.

Above: **The Ring of Brodgar, or "Circle of the Sun," an ancient stone circle near Maes Howe. Today 27 out of the 60 standing stones remain.**

Opposite: **Details of markings on a Celtic gravestone found on Iona Island.**

ROMANS, VIKINGS, AND CELTS

When the Romans ventured to Scotland around A.D. 80, they discovered a country where a number of Celtic tribes fought one another and farmed the inhospitable land. The inhabitants grew oats and barley and hunted deer and salmon. Since they had tattoos, the Romans named them Picts, which comes from the Latin *pictus*, meaning "painted."

The Roman invasion was led by Agricola, the governor of Britain. He drove the Picts into the Highlands and built a series of stone forts on the land between the Firth of Forth and Firth of Clyde, which is the narrowest point between the eastern and western shores. It was not until the second century that a more permanent defense force was established along Hadrian's Wall. Named after the Roman Emperor Hadrian, the wall was designed to keep the Picts out of England, an easier task than subduing them. A second wall was built 20 years later by Emperor Antoninus Pius, but it was rapidly abandoned. It is estimated that during the Romans' 300-year stay in Scotland, 50,000 soldiers died guarding the border.

The Romans withdrew from Britain at the turn of the fifth century, leaving Scotland occupied by four tribes. The Picts staked their claim on the northern islands of Scotland and the north and east of the mainland. In the southwest were the Romanized Britons. The west of Scotland was colonized by the Scots, a tribe from northern Ireland. The southeast was controlled by the Angles, who came from across the North Sea.

At the end of the eighth century another new culture influenced Scottish life—the Vikings. They first invaded all of the northern islands and then the northeast of mainland Scotland. The Shetland and Orkney Islands became the base for a Viking culture that spread to England and Ireland.

For several centuries the Celtic tribes fought among themselves for control of Scotland. But the Scots and Picts came together in A.D. 843 when Kenneth I MacAlpin, king of the Scots, became the king of the Picts. The lands north of the Clyde and Forth Rivers came under his control. In 1018 Scots king Malcolm II defeated the Angles and took over their territories. By 1034 the kingdom of the Picts, Scots, Angles, and Britons became one.

Left: **A woodprint showing Celts in everyday life. The Celts had a highly structured social system, which was divided into king, warrior aristocracy, and freemen farmers.**

Opposite: **Roman soldiers dressed for war. The first recorded battle in Scottish history was the Battle of Mons Graupius, in northeastern Scotland, between the Romans and Picts in A.D. 84. The Romans won and drove the Picts into the mountains.**

Above: **Robert the Bruce (right) attacking Sir Henry de Bohun at the Battle of Bannockburn in 1314. Bruce led 6,000 men against 20,000 English forces and defeated them.**

THE MIDDLE AGES

Scottish kings were not chosen by direct succession but by a system known as tanistry, where any male in the four-generation family could be the king's successor. This led to murder and mayhem as eligible contestants vied for the throne. The most famous was Macbeth's murder of Duncan I in the year 1040, freely retold in William Shakespeare's play, *Macbeth*. Unlike the story in the play, however, Macbeth was a successful king according to historical accounts.

Malcolm III Canmore, who killed and succeeded Macbeth, established a dynasty based on succession through the male line. His heirs also replaced the Scottish clan system with the English system of feudalism, where loyal followers of the king were bestowed plots of land. The feudal system was implemented successfully in southern Scotland, but in the Highlands the clan system was never eradicated. Two cultures thus developed in Scotland, a Gaelic-speaking and clan-based culture in the Highlands and a Scots-speaking feudal system in the south.

In 1290 the Scottish throne fell vacant, and Edward I of England was asked to choose a successor. The two main contenders were the sixth Robert the Bruce and John Balliol. Edward chose Balliol, and in exchange for his favor, demanded homage from him. Scotland was made a vassal state of England. In 1295 Balliol renounced his allegiance to England and formed an alliance with France, known as the Auld Alliance. A year later Edward I deposed and executed Balliol. He also incurred the wrath of the Scots by removing the Stone of Destiny, used in the coronation of Scottish kings. Resistance to English rule grew, led by Sir William Wallace. In 1306 the eighth Robert the Bruce crowned himself king of Scotland. In 1314 there was a decisive battle at Bannockburn, south of Stirling, when the English troops of Edward II were defeated and driven out of Scotland by Bruce's army. In 1320 Bruce's supporters petitioned the pope in the Declaration of Arbroath, and Bruce was declared king of Scotland. Eight years later England's Edward III granted independence to Scotland.

SIR WILLIAM WALLACE

Scottish hero William Wallace was the son of a knight. He fought for freedom from English rule and raised an army of peasants, lesser nobles, and townspeople, all angry at the injustices perpetrated on the Scottish people. Sir William had one successful battle with the English at Stirling Bridge in 1297. He took over Stirling Castle and returned to Scotland, where he was knighted. The following year his troops were wiped out by the English army at the Battle of Falkirk at Stirling, and Wallace fled to France. On August 5, 1305, he was arrested near Glasgow. Wallace was taken to London where he was hung, drawn, and quartered. His mutilated body was put on display. It was said that his quarters were sent to Newcastle, Berwick, Sterling, and Perth. Wallace was portrayed by Mel Gibson in the 1995 Oscar-winning movie *Braveheart*.

Mary Stewart or Stuart (French form) was said to have faced her execution with quiet dignity. Her body was laid to rest in Westminister Abbey.

MARY QUEEN OF SCOTS

After independence a few centuries of weak kings and regencies followed. The big families of Scotland again fought for power. This came to a head in the reign of Mary Queen of Scots, who was crowned as a Catholic monarch in 1542 when she was six days old. Mary was supposed to marry the heir of England's King Henry VIII, but when the Scottish regents rejected the plan, Henry VIII invaded Scotland.

The regents turned to France, who expelled the English. Mary was sent to France at age five and brought up in the French court. In 1558 Mary married the French dauphin, Francis. She returned to Scotland three years later, after the death of her husband, and found a very different country. During the time she was away, the Reformation had taken place, and Scotland was no longer a Catholic country. Mass was forbidden, and the authority of the Pope was no longer recognized. Church lands had been confiscated by the nobles, and John Knox was proposing that Scotland did not need a monarch.

In 1565 Mary married her cousin, Henry Darnley, who was murdered two years later. Shortly after, Mary married James Hepburn, the prime suspect in Darnley's murder. In 1567 Mary was forced to abdicate in favor of her son and was imprisoned in a castle on Loch Leven in central Scotland. She escaped to England and sought refuge with her cousin, Elizabeth I. Fearing that Mary could be a threat to the English throne, Elizabeth I imprisoned her for the next 18 years. In 1587 Mary was executed at Fortheringhay Castle in Northamptonshire, England.

THE 17TH CENTURY

Mary was succeeded in 1603 by her son James VI, who was raised as a Protestant. He became James I of England and temporarily united the two countries. Once established in England, James passed laws bringing bishops back to the Scottish church, thus making himself more powerful since he appointed them. His son, Charles I, made matters much worse. He imposed the High Anglican form of worship on the Church of Scotland. This provoked thousands to sign a pledge called the National Covenant in 1638 to maintain the Presbyterian prayer service. A crisis developed, and the Covenanters recruited a huge army. Unable to muster troops of his own without money, Charles called on the English Parliament, which he hoped would agree to raise taxes for an army. Instead, it criticized Charles' rule, and in 1642 he declared war on his own parliament. Both sides asked for the assistance of the Scottish Parliament, and it sided with the English Parliament. The parliamentary armies, led by Oliver Cromwell, captured Charles I. He was executed by the English in 1649. But the two allies soon fell out: the Scots wanted rule by the church, and the English rule by parliament. Cromwell invaded Scotland and seized power; and the country was ruled by commissioners established by the English Parliament.

When Charles II was restored to the throne in 1660, he compromised with the Scottish church leaders. After the bishops were reinstated, they never interfered with the running of the church and local government. James II of England, who came to the throne in 1685, was a Catholic. He incurred the wrath of the Protestants and was deposed in 1689. He was replaced by his nephew and son-in-law, William of Orange, who was a Protestant. In Scotland the bishops were abolished again, but William was careful not to give the Presbyterian church back its political power. Control of the state remained with the Scottish Parliament.

James II of England antagonized the Scottish Parliament by asking it to be more tolerant toward the Catholics.

Above: **A plaque commemorating the Battle of Culloden. Even though the battle lasted only 40 minutes, it changed centuries of Highland customs.**

Opposite: **A Highlanders' meeting at Stafford House to protest against the change in the tartans of the Highland regiments.**

THE ACT OF UNION

Although the accession of William of Orange calmed much of the dispute between the Scottish church and English state, things were still not resolved. William's reign was dominated by war with France, an old ally of Scotland in its efforts to maintain independence. Scots paid taxes and fought against France in the war, and trade between Scotland and France was ruined. Another incident made matters worse. The Bank of England and a group of Scottish merchants formed a trading company in Panama. The venture was a disaster and Scotland nearly became bankrupt. Riots against the English broke out in Scottish towns.

England followed a policy of keeping a tight hold on Scotland. When William's successor Anne died childless, the English Parliament suggested that Sophie of Hanover ascend the throne. In exchange they would give trade concessions to Scotland. In 1707 the Act of Union was passed, uniting the English and Scottish parliaments. This was bitterly opposed by the Highlanders, and there were several rebellions known as the Jacobite uprisings in 1708, 1715, 1719, and 1745 to replace Hanoverian rule.

The rebellions culminated in the Battle of Culloden in 1746 led by Charles Edward Stuart (Bonnie Prince Charlie), the heir to the deposed James II. As many as 1,200 Jacobites were killed, and Prince Charlie fled to France. The English government issued a ban on wearing tartans, playing bagpipes, and bearing arms. This ban was called the Disarming Act. Those who led the rebellions lost their land, and private armies were made illegal. This effectively brought the Scottish clan system to an end.

HIGHLAND CLEARANCES

For centuries the clan system had encouraged a large population in Scotland. Clan chiefs needed large armies to fight their battles, and they rewarded their supporters with land. Once the clan system was dismantled in the 18th century, the chiefs who had not had their estates confiscated no longer needed to lease their lands. It became more profitable to turn them over to sheep farming.

The clan chiefs came up with various solutions to evict their tenants. Some people were encouraged to emigrate; thousands of Scots went to the United States and Canada in the early 19th century. Some were forced out of their land—the worst of the Highland clearances was that by the Countess of Sutherland who had had 15,000 people brutally thrown out of their homes between 1805 and 1821. Some were moved to smallholdings called crofts.

The crofters eked out a living as small tenant farmers on marginal lands until the end of the 19th century when falling prices meant that they could no longer pay their rents. The crofters formed organizations aimed at resisting eviction and succeeded in getting reforms to the system. The number of crofters in the Scottish Highlands continue to decline in the 20th century.

THE INDUSTRIAL REVOLUTION

Similar to the rest of Britain, Scotland's industrial revolution depended on the trade of American and West Indian cotton and tobacco. Glasgow was particularly suited to this trade, being located on the west coast of Scotland. The journey to America was convenient, and there was a large pool of people to provide a workforce. A cotton processing industry developed with mass production techniques in large factories.

The need for mechanization encouraged the iron industry, which in turn fueled the coal industry. Scotland had plenty of iron and coal. Trade fostered a shipbuilding industry that strengthened both iron and coal works, as steam driven ships were developed. The population drifted toward the centers of industry in the lowlands. Glasgow grew rapidly, leading to the development of urban overcrowding in tenement buildings with little or no sanitation. The Irish, fleeing from a famine, swelled the urban population. Many workers, such as coalminers, suffered terrible hardship with no organized labor movements to protect them and no right to vote.

In the early part of the century several attempts to organize the workers ended in mass arrests and deportations to Australia. The 1832 Reform Bill extended the right to vote to the middle class, which made the lives of the poorer classes harder, with less support from the better-off. The rich merchants grew prosperous, while specialized workers such as engineers became well-off. A socialist movement developed in Scotland affiliated with similar groups in England, but little improvement was made in the well-being of the poor.

Above: **A worker at the National Cash Register Company plant in Dundee. When the plant was established, jobs were provided for men and women of many backgrounds—jute mill workers, general laborers, machine shop workers, and shop clerks.**

Opposite: **A small procession escorts the Stone of Destiny over the Tweed Bridge at Coldstream, just across the England-Scotland border. The stone is on its way to Edinburgh Castle.**

THE STONE OF DESTINY

The Stone of Destiny has long been accorded magical powers. It is believed to be the stone on which Jacob rested his head when he dreamed of a ladder to heaven. The stone was revered wherever it was taken. In the early years of Christianity the stone traveled to Ireland and was brought from there to Dunadd, capital of Dalriada, the ancient kingdom of the Scots, by missionaries. It became the coronation seat of the Scottish kings, each chieftain bringing a little earth from his own kingdom to place in a depression in the rock on which the king sat.

In the ninth century it was carried to Scone, two miles northeast of Perth. Edward I heard of its magical powers and in 1296 had it taken to Westminster Abbey in London and placed under the coronation throne so that English monarchs would get the benefit of the magic. But the wily Scots must have tricked Edward since the stone he had carried to England was a plain piece of sandstone, and it is known that the original Stone of Destiny was ornately carved. The stone stayed in Westminister Abbey for 700 years until 1950 when some Scottish nationalists stole it. Three months later it turned up in the ruins of Arbroath Abbey. In 1996 an ailing Conservative government in Britain, trying to gain favor with the Scottish electorate that had largely voted against them, returned the stone to Edinburgh. But the Scots did not want it. They knew it was a fake. The real Stone of Destiny, according to legend, is hidden in a Scottish hillside and will be returned by its guardians to Scone when the time is right.

A war memorial in Glasgow to Scottish soldiers who died during World War I and World War II. Around 74,000 Scots lost their lives in World War I and 40,000 in the World War II.

WORLD WAR I AND WORLD WAR II

World War I damaged the prosperity of Scottish industry. Trade with America stopped. The shipbuilding industry, in particular, did not recover from the effects of changing trade patterns. Scotland suffered some of the worst social conditions in the United Kingdom. This led to the highest infant mortality rate in Europe. Socialist groups grew in strength, and in 1922, 22 members of the Scottish Labor Party were elected to parliament.

As the world entered the economic slump of the 1930s, Scotland suffered badly, and emigration to America increased. It was estimated that 400,000, or 10% of the population, left the country between 1921 and 1931. By 1936 the annual output of the shipyards had fallen from 738,000 tons

(750,000 metric tons) to less than 59,040 tons (60,000 metric tons). Two-thirds of the workforce were unemployed. In this atmosphere of poverty and depression, the only hope for most working-class people was a mix of socialism and nationalism.

World War II put an end to the depression in Scotland. The shipbuilding industry revived, stimulating coal mining and other war-related industries. Relatively untouched by the war, Scotland prospered until World War II ended, when demand for ships and armaments stopped. In the following years Scotland benefited, along with the rest of Britain, from the massive social changes taking place—free healthcare reduced the infant mortality rate, education improved, privately owned industries were nationalized, and a massive rebuilding program began. Scotland, like the rest of Britain, experienced competition from newly emerging Third World countries, and Scottish industry declined until the discovery of North Sea oil in the 1970s. The find resurrected the economy and provided jobs for thousands.

By the end of the 1970s the old industries of Scotland were moribund, and more and more people began to believe that Scotland's future lay in independence. A referendum was held in 1979: 33% of the voters chose independence, 31% chose to remain part of Britain, and the rest did not vote. Although a majority of those who voted wanted independence, the overall vote for independence was not high enough, and Scotland remained a part of Britain. Scotland benefited little during the years when Margaret Thatcher was prime minister of England.

After the 1992 elections there were only a small number of Scottish Conservative party members in the British Parliament, so Scotland found itself ruled by a government it largely had not elected. The sense of alienation grew. Devolution, as the process of returning self-government to Scotland has been called, finally took place in 1999.

When World War II broke out, Clydeside shipyards started construction on warships and engineering firms began making arms and ammunition. The west-central region of Scotland became indispensable. Aware of this fact, the Germans bombed Clydeside on March 13 and 14, 1941, killing 1,000 people and injuring 1,500.

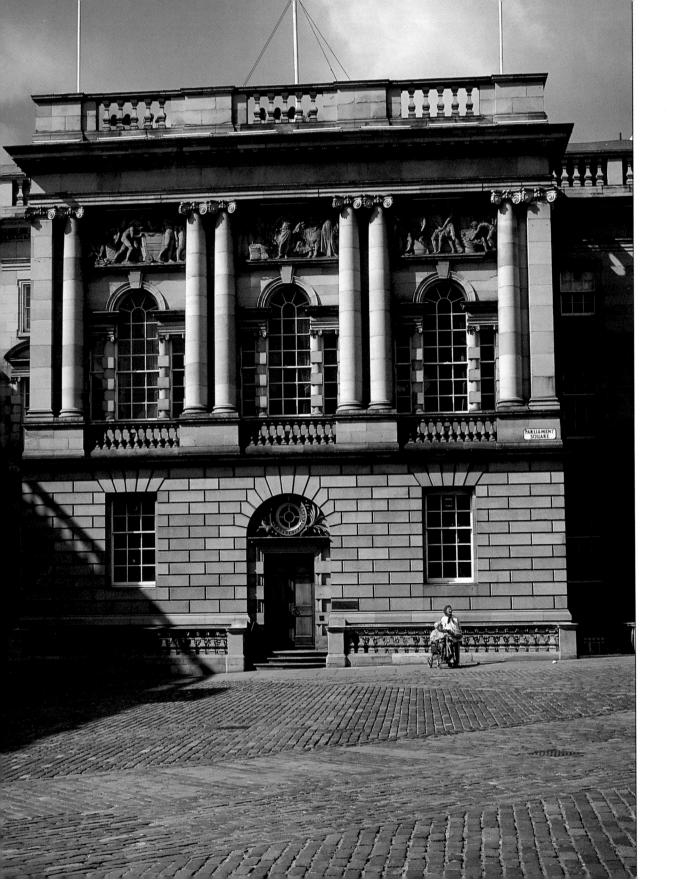

GOVERNMENT

SCOTLAND ELECTED A PARLIAMENT in 1999 for the first time in 300 years. In 1707 an Act of Union abolished the Scottish Parliament and combined both the English and Scottish parliaments. In the 20th century responsibility for Scotland was gradually handed over to the Scottish Office, which was based in Edinburgh since 1939 and overseen by the secretary of state for Scotland, also a member of the British cabinet. In the 1960s talk began of a devolved government for Scotland, but a referendum held in 1979 did not gather the 40% majority required for this to take place.

The change came in 1997 with the election of a New Labor government in Britain committed to devolution in both Scotland and Wales. Their proposal for Scotland was a limited form of self-government with a parliament with powers to legislate and levy taxes. A referendum was held in 1997: 74.3% voted for the establishment of a Scottish Parliament, while 53.5% of the voters were in favor of the power to levy and vary taxes.

Left: **A voter in Highland gear outside a polling station during the 1999 Scottish elections.**

Opposite: **Parliament Square in Edinburgh.**

THE PARLIAMENT

For the 1999 election a system of proportional representation was used, unlike in the rest of Britain. This meant that no overall majority was won by any party, and all shades of opinion would be represented in the Scottish Parliament.

Under an arrangement between two Scottish parties, the Liberal Democrats and the New Labor Party, at least half of the election candidates were women. In the election for the Scottish Parliament in May 1999, 48 of the 129 members elected to parliament were women. Only two other countries, Denmark and Sweden, have a higher proportion of women as members of parliament.

Scottish first minister, Donald Dewar, greets Queen Elizabeth on the day of the official opening of the Scottish Parliament.

The Scottish Parliament first met in January 2000. It has powers over local government, business assistance, health, education, housing, social work, agriculture, and food policy—areas where Scottish people believed that a government based in London, with little understanding of the needs of people hundreds of miles away, could not always judge correctly what decisions to make. The parliament has a budget of about US$22 billion and can raise taxes, for example a Scotland-only tax to implement social reform or education policy in the country.

The British Parliament in London retains control over employment law, economic and monetary policy and taxation, social security benefits and pensions, passports and immigration, negotiations with the European Union, and foreign affairs.

The new parliament building is to be constructed near Holyrood Palace in Edinburgh and will cost US$128 million.

The Scottish Parliament's temporary home is in a part of Edinburgh known as The Mound.

THE SCOTTISH OFFICE

The Scottish Office is a department of the government in London that has special responsibility for Scottish affairs. The head of the department is the secretary of state for Scotland, who has authority over Scottish legal services, the Scottish record office, the prison service, and the courts. Other areas of interest are agriculture and fisheries, a regional development office, and education and industry. It is in most of these areas that the new Scottish Parliament has been given authority, so the future will see a balance of power between the Scottish Office and Scottish Parliament.

The Scottish Office is based in St. Andrew's House in Edinburgh as well as in London. As the Scottish Parliament evolves, the secretary of state for Scotland will no longer be needed, and its responsibilities will be taken over by the chief minister of the Scottish Parliament.

Balmoral Castle where the queen stays when she is in Scotland. The original castle was bought by Queen Victoria and Prince Albert in 1852 and replaced by this Scottish baronial design building.

LOCAL GOVERNMENT

Local government in Scotland has also undergone considerable reorganization. Before 1975 Scotland was divided into counties, and the larger cities were governed by city corporations. The old counties are still used as the basis of land registration in Scotland. Between 1975 and 1995 there were nine regional authorities, divided into 53 district councils, and three unitary island councils. In 1996 the local government in Scotland was reorganized into 29 unitary authorities, although the three island authorities have been retained. Each local government body is run by a series of councilors who are elected every four years.

THE QUEEN

Scotland has no president and is still part of the United Kingdom, so Queen Elizabeth is the head of state, head of the judiciary, and commander in chief of the armed forces. All acts of parliament require the queen's assent, and it is she who confers peerages and other honors. These are largely technicalities and are carried out by the government in London with Queen Elizabeth's consent. The queen lives for part of the year at Balmoral Castle in eastern Scotland.

THE JUDICIARY

At the union of Scotland and England in 1707, Scottish law was not brought into line with English law, so Scotland has always had its own set of laws and judicial system. One way in which the Scottish legal system differs from the British is that a criminal proceeding can be brought against anyone from the age of 8 onward; in Britain the minimum age is 10. Another difference is that at the end of a trial the verdict can be "guilty," "not guilty," or "not proven." The last is known as the "Scotch verdict."

Deputy first minister, Henry McLeish, being sworn in at the Court of Session in Edinburgh in May 1999.

The ministers who are responsible for judicial affairs are the lord advocate and solicitor general (called the attorney general in the United States). They give advice to the Scottish government on legal matters and help to formulate legislation.

In Scotland the most serious criminal cases, which involve murder, rape, and grave drug offences, are tried in the High Court of Justiciary. Civil cases that involve challenging government decisions are heard in the Court of Session. The Court of Session, which is made up of the lord president, lord justice clerk, and 22 other judges, is divided into the Inner House and the Outer House. Minor civil and criminal cases are heard in the sheriff courts and district courts.

POLITICAL PARTIES

Scotland has four major parties and several smaller ones. The three parties that dominate British politics also dominate Scottish politics.

NEW LABOR PARTY has dominated Scotland's political scene for several years, long before it came to power in Britain. Its policies are dubbed a "third way;" it supposedly avoids the class-ridden party politics characteristic of British politics in the 20th century. The party has a massive majority in Britain and is often accused of undermining the parliamentary system by sidelining the role of parliament as a ratifying body in favor of cabinet decisions. It was responsible for initiating devolution for Scotland in 1999.

An animated conference hosted by the Scottish Nationalist Party to garner support for full independence for Scotland.

SCOTTISH NATIONALIST PARTY The next most popular party in Scotland was formed in 1934 and is the youngest of the leading political groups. Until the 1960s they were unsuccessful, getting less than 1% of the national vote. After the failure of the devolution referendum in 1977, they lost the few seats in parliament that they had. The 1980s were also difficult as support for the Labor Party grew. Finally, in the 1990s they became the second most powerful party in Scotland.

The Scottish Nationalist Party is led by Alex Salmond and has adopted policies of a social democratic nature that are slightly left of center. The party would prefer a much more powerful Scottish Parliament, capable of levying taxes as it chose and having some say in international affairs. They enjoy considerable support across a wide range of Scottish people.

A New Labor Party billboard. The party won a landslide victory in the 1997 elections and the Labor government led by prime minister Tony Blair called for devolution for Scotland.

CONSERVATIVE PARTY Least popular of the big British parties is the Conservative Party, which after the election in 1997, had no representatives in the British Parliament, no majority in any local council, and no member in the European Parliament. Although the party's profile in Scotland is large, it wield almost no power there. The referendum for devolution was opposed by the Conservatives. Since the referendum's success and the establishment of the Scottish Parliament, they have committed themselves to the idea and have formed a separate Scottish Conservative Party.

GREEN PARTY Another party represented under the proportional representation system is the Green Party, a European-wide movement that focuses on issues concerning the environment.

ECONOMY

AS A MEMBER of the United Kingdom, Scotland is part of a flourishing British economy, where service industries such as financial services and insurance are on the increase; one in 10 people is setting up a small business; unemployment is at its lowest in 20 years; and inflation is satisfactorily low. Take Scotland out of the larger context, and the picture is not quite so rosy.

Like other heavily industrialized areas of Britain, central Scotland suffered massive unemployment as coal mining, steel making, shipbuilding, and engineering industries closed down after World War II. The discovery of offshore oil in the North Sea in the 1970s offset this slump for some time, but that industry too is in decline as the oil fields empty out. But traditional industries such as woolen and tweed production and whisky distilling still survive. Presently, Scotland's economic future seems to lie in the electronics, finance and service industries, food production and fishing, and tourism.

Left: **Tourists enjoying a popular Ghost Walk tour in Edinburgh. Taking place in the evenings, the tour guide, usually dressed as a character from horror movies, brings visitors around places in the city that are said to be haunted.**

Opposite: **A man carefully examines the quality of the whisky in the oak barrels. After distillation, the spirit is left to mature in the barrels for at least three years.**

An engineering plant in Glasgow. Efforts have recently been made to replace labor-intensive heavy industries with high-technology enterprises.

HEAVY INDUSTRY

At the peak of production for shipbuilding, coal mining, steel production, and engineering in the early 20th century, the Central Lowlands of Scotland became the world's most heavily industrialized area. Glasgow was the center of activity, and Glaswegians called their city the "second city in the empire." Industries in Glasgow and its satellite towns produced one-fifth of Britain's steel, one-third of its shipping tonnage, half the marine horse power, a third of railroad rolling stock, and almost all the sewing machines.

Like other manufacturing areas, Scotland's cities suffered as technology changed, and big engineering projects became rarer. The steel industry became less profitable and closed down, while reserves of coal declined until working the mines became unprofitable. Only opencast mining is carried out in Scotland now. A boom in the engineering industry came when North Sea oil was discovered, and several Scottish firms developed new skills in oil rig manufacture that have been used both off the coast of Scotland and abroad.

OFFSHORE OIL AND GAS

In the 1970s oil and gas fields were discovered in the North Sea off the east coast of Scotland. Aberdeen became a base for the offshore oil rigs that litter the northeast continental shelf. In the 1970s and 1980s Aberdeen grew rapidly to accommodate the administrative areas of the industry, house workers, and provide helicopter services. Then from 1985 to 1986 the price of oil collapsed and with it the economy of the city. Prices have recovered since then.

An oil rig in the North Sea. Scotland receives a small percentage of revenue from oil, which largely goes into the British Treasury.

In 1999 there were 173 offshore fields in production, and more were being explored in remote areas of the continental shelf. Since the first field opened in 1970, Scotland has produced more than 1.97 billion tons (2 billion metric tons) of oil. The most productive fields have been Forties, Brent, Ninian, and Piper, off the northeast coast.

Reserves in the North Sea are estimated to be nearly 3.35 billion tons (3.4 billion metric tons), and the industry is expected to keep producing oil in the 21st century. There are also one or two onshore oil fields, but their production scale is small.

The interior of a bank. Scottish banks have expanded to North America and Europe. During the 19th century, much of the development of the American west was financed by Scottish banks, in areas such as mining, railroads, and ranching.

ELECTRONICS

Scotland has a small electronics industry, known as Silicon Glen, found in the region between Glasgow and Edinburgh. It employs about 40,000 people and produces about 13% of Europe's silicon conductors, 35% of the personal computers, 45% of the computer workstations, and 50% of the automated teller machines (ATMs). Companies that have invested in the electronics industry include Compaq, Digital, Hughes, IBM, and NEC.

FINANCE

Scotland has three major banks, the Bank of Scotland, the Royal Bank of Scotland, and the Clydesdale Bank. All three issue their own bank notes that are legal tender in Scotland only. Since the mid-1960s, Edinburgh has become an important financial and business center, second only to London in the United Kingdom. Other banking services that have developed in Scotland are mutual funds and investment trusts, which now represent a third of all such trusts in Britain.

FISHING

Fishing is an important part of Scotland's economy, but its prospects for expansion are affected by the European Union's restrictions on catches as well as declining fish stocks in Scottish waters. Because there are fishing quotas for each fishing vessel, fishermen have to throw away any excess fish they catch. A fisheries police force enforces these quotas, and ships are often boarded for inspection. In 1996, 66 fishermen were prosecuted for overfishing.

Two-thirds of the British catch comes from ships registered and based in Scottish ports. The bulk of fish brought into these ports are cod, haddock, herring, mackerel, and sole, chiefly white fish. Peterhead, in northeast Scotland, is the European Union's largest white fish port and produces annual catches valued at more than US$75 million, making this town and its population of 18,000 one of the richest in Scotland. The Grampian region of Scotland is one of Britain's main fish processing centers.

Fishermen unloading crabs at a pier.

Shellfish are also an important industry in Scotland, and scallop, lobster, langoustine, and crab are major sources of income. They are caught in the wild and raised on fish farms. The chief areas for shellfish farming are in the Highlands and Islands. Turnover in 1996 was US$362 million. Around 3,000 people are employed in shellfish farming.

Oysters, mussels, and clams are also farmed. In addition, 83,121 tons of salmon are raised in Scotland each year, the largest amount among the member countries in the European Union, and 43,635 tons of trout with a value of US$351 million are also sold.

Farmers rounding up sheep to separate the yearlings, which would be sold at a sheep auction.

AGRICULTURE

Agriculture in Scotland has both benefited and lost from the advances in mechanization since the 1950s when 88,000 people were employed on the land. Today only around 30,000 people are employed in agriculture, many of them casual laborers and part-time workers. In the Southern Uplands and Highlands, sheep farming dominates, while in the southwest, with better drained and more accessible lands, dairy farming is more important. The eastern seaboard supports the farming of barley, potatoes, rapeseed, wheat, and oats. Silage and hay, as well as root vegetables, are produced as animal feed. Areas in the north of Scotland, such as Argyle and Bute in the western Grampians, the Outer Hebrides, and the Orkney and Shetland

Islands, are dominated by tiny farms known as crofts. Few croft farmers can make a living, and many crofts have been abandoned.

FORESTRY

About 15% of Scotland is covered in forest. The forests are maintained by the forestry commission and private landowners. Both natural woodland and planted pine forests are maintained and expanded, and timber provides a significant income to the country. Farmed forests include Scots pine, larch, and Douglas fir. The European Union has designated some Highland forests a "class one" habitat, meaning that they must be protected and developed as habitats for wildlife.

Copper-pot stills are used to distill the fermented solution of malted barley and hot water.

OTHER INDUSTRIES

Other industries in Scotland that have contributed significantly to the national economy are traditional enterprises such as whiskey and tweeds manufacturing, and tourism, the biggest revenue earner.

DISTILLING The distilling industry has always been a part of Scottish economic life. Scotch whisky accounts for 27% of British production, and there are 92 distilleries in Scotland, which produce either malt or grain whisky. In the first, malted barley is used, while in the second a mixture of ordinary barley and other grains. Most Scotch whisky available is made from a blend of these two. About 13,000 people work in the industry, and another 55,000 work in associated industries such as grain production and transport. Ninety percent of the production is exported to the United States, Japan, and the European Union. Most of the distilleries are in the

Speyside district in eastern Scotland, and well-known brands such as Chivas Regal, Bell's, Teacher's, and Johnnie Walker are made from blends from this area.

HARRIS TWEED Another small but important export is Harris tweed, which is produced in the Inner and Outer Hebrides. This was once a cottage industry, the tweed handmade by women in their homes from the wool of the sheep they reared themselves. The wool was washed, dyed, spun, and "waulked" or beaten smooth by one woman and her family or friends, but this is no longer the case. The cloth is now produced commercially, and the business employs about 400 millworkers and 650 weavers. But authentic Harris tweed is that made in the Outer Hebrides from pure Scottish wool. Today the chief work is done on Lewis Island. Some traditions remain. The cloth is still dyed using local materials—a wild plant called broom produces yellow, heather makes green, and oak and iris give black.

The manufacturing of Harris tweed is now a much faster process, thanks to mechanization.

TOURISM Scotland's other major industry is tourism, with Edinburgh second only to London as a popular tourist destination in Britain. Most of Scotland's tourists come from other parts of Britain or Scotland itself, many for the winter sports to be enjoyed there or the abundance of walking trails and other outdoor sports. Over a million people visit Scotland from abroad each year.

MINERALS Scotland also produces some minerals in small amounts. Marble is quarried in the northwest, and barites is mined in the Highlands.

SCOTS

THE SCOTTISH PEOPLE are a mix of the various ancient tribes that invaded the country and a modern influx of people that migrated from other parts of Britain and farther afield. The population is around 5.2 million, and its growth rate has fallen slightly every year since 1995 after a period of increase in the early 1990s. Overall, the average age is increasing, similar to other western European countries with aging populations. The birth rate is 11.2 per thousand. In 1998 the number of live births in Scotland was 57,319, the lowest since records began in 1855. Forty-four percent of these were to mothers over 30, and 39% of them were born to parents who were not married. Life expectancy for men is 73 and 78 for women. Some areas of Scotland show an increase in their population, such as Dundee, Orkney, and Falkirk and East Lothian in eastern Scotland. Glasgow has the highest increase, while the biggest fall in population has been in Aberdeen.

Left: **A smiling young woman disproves the belief that the Scots are a dour and sour people.**

Opposite: **A boy discovering if Scotsmen wear anything under their kilts.**

THE CELTS, PICTS, AND SCOTS

Around 500 B.C. the Celtic tribes moved into Scotland from the south, where they had already colonized England and Wales. They spoke a language of European origin, which is linked to modern-day Welsh and Breton.

By about the fifth century A.D. there were five distinct ethnic and linguistic groups in Scotland—the Picts, about whom very little is known; the Angles in the southeast of the country; the Britons in the southwest (the latter two groups being invaders from England); the Dalriadic Scots, who first established themselves in Argyll, western Scotland; and the Norse people in the northern islands and north and east of the Scottish mainland.

The Dalriadic Scots are the real ancestors of Scottish culture. These warriors came by boat from Ireland and

A hand-colored print of a Norseman. Armies of Norse warriors would raid towns and cities along the European coasts from the 9th to 11th centuries.

gradually took over the whole country by force and assimilation. Legend says that the first Scots to arrive in Scotland were a family called MacErc. They assumed control over an area they called Dalriada after their homeland in Ireland. One of their ancestors was said to have married an Egyptian princess called Scot, and the name that they (and eventually the whole country) adopted is hers.

MODERN SCOTLAND

Over the centuries the Picts and Scots merged into one Gaelic-speaking community, but other groups have contributed to the ethnic diversity of the country. In the 19th century many Irish arrived in Scotland, fleeing a terrible famine in Ireland. Industrial development attracted workers from the north of England, and in the second half of the 20th century, ethnic

minorities from even farther afield settled in Scotland. It is estimated that about 64,000 people of different ethnicities live in Scotland. Slightly over 1% of the population, this is a much lower figure than for the whole of Britain, where West Indians, Indians, Chinese, and other ethnic groups have settled in far larger numbers.

The ethnic minorities in Scotland include Indians, Pakistanis, and Chinese, most of whom have migrated from other parts of Britain. They are relatively young: a third are under 15 years of age. About 60% live in Strathclyde (northwest of the Southern Uplands), 20% in Lothian (western Central Lowlands), and smaller numbers in Tayside (central Scotland), Grampian, and Fife (eastern Central Lowlands). Another distinct cultural, if not ethnic, group in Scotland, are Gaelic-speakers who make up about 1.3% of the population. About a third of Gaelic-speakers live in the central belt of Scotland.

Scotland has a rich melting pot of people from different parts of the world.

There are around 25 million people of Scottish origin outside the country, compared to a population of five million in Scotland.

Scottish-born Alexander Bell testing the telephone, which he invented in 1876 in the United States.

SCOTTISH LEGENDS

Robert ("Rob Roy") MacGregor (1671–1734), a pirate and cattle raider from the Trossachs, an area east and northeast of Loch Lomond, fought in the Jacobite wars against the English. His clan, the MacGregors, gave us the word "blackmail" from their habit of demanding a tax of black meal from the local villagers for protection. Many years after Roy's death, his story was immortalized by Sir Walter Scott, and he became a romantic Robin Hood-type figure. He was glamorized even further in the 1995 Hollywood movie *Rob Roy*, which starred Liam Neeson.

Another Scot who has passed into legend is Flora MacDonald (1722–1790), who sheltered Bonnie Prince Charlie when he escaped the English in his flight through Scotland. She dressed him as her maid Betty Burke when she might have claimed a reward of £30,000. Later she emigrated to the United States where her family sided with the British during the War of Independence. Flora MacDonald returned to Scotland in 1778.

FAMOUS SCOTS

In science and engineering, Scotland has produced many famous people. James Watt (1736–1819) modified the steam engine, and his improvements led to its being used widely. Watt also did a lot of research into electricity. John Macadam (1756–1836) gave his name to the material that surfaces roads. Thomas Telford (1757–1834), a shepherd's son, was an engineer who built the Dean Bridge in Edinburgh, the Caledonian canal that links the two coasts of Scotland, and the Gotha canal in Sweden. Charles MacIntosh (1776–1843) invented a waterproof material; James Young (1811–1889) was the first chemist to refine oil commercially; James Clerk Maxwell (1831–1879) proposed the notions of cybernetics and electromagnetism and took the world's first color photograph; and John Dunlop (1840–1921) invented the pneumatic tire.

Sir Alexander Flemming, who discovered penicillin, won the Nobel Prize for medicine in 1945.

The 20th century saw more important Scottish inventors. Sir James Dewar (1842–1923) created the vacuum flask, Alexander Graham Bell (1847–1922), a Scot who emigrated to the United States, invented the telephone, and Sir Alexander Fleming (1881–1955) discovered penicillin in 1928, although the drug took another 11 years to perfect. Other Scots who have given great inventions to the world include John Logie Baird (1888–1946), who invented an early form of television, and Marie Stopes (1880–1950), a pioneer in modern birth control methods and founder of the world's first birth control clinic. She was also an advocate of women's rights and the first woman to be appointed to the staff of Manchester University. In 1996 the world was informed that Scottish embryologists had successfully cloned a sheep, Dolly, from the cells of an adult sheep.

THE CLANS AND TARTANS

The word, "clan" comes from the Gaelic clann, *which means "children." Each clan member takes the name of the chief, regardless of whether they are related by blood or sworn to allegiance.*

Now a romantic shadow of its former self, the clan system once regulated Scottish life. Scotland was divided into clans, which were extended families and their dependents who all served one chief and in exchange received his protection. The chief could call on his clan members to fight in wars or work in the fields. In exchange, each member of the clan could expect to have his home, crops, and family well looked after. The clans often fought one another over land and sovereignty, and there were many mergers of clans. They were united for a time against the English, but the clan system was banned in 1746.

Each clan was identified by its name and tartan, or the patterned cloth that the men wore. Originally, this was one large piece of cloth worn both as a skirt and coat and belted at the waist. It was made of fine wool spun in the village, and each man wore the same pattern, not because it was a uniform but because of its origin—one village might know how to make blue dye, while another might be better at yellow. The colors were natural and soft and merged into one another, the better ones acting as camouflage. The cloth was also waterproof.

After 1746 most tartan was banned for almost 40 years, long enough for the women who made it to grow old and the skills to be lost. Not all tartans were banned however: the Highland regiments wore the government tartan—the Black Watch pattern. In the early 19th century, when Sir Walter Scott's novels romanticizing Highland life became popular and King George IV chose to wear a skirt patterned in strong striped and checked colors, wearing tartans gained popularity. Clans that had long forgotten what their tartan was, invented one to sell to the English.

When modern tourists, descended from Scottish emigrants, visit Scotland today and ask for their family tartan, the cloth they are sold has

very little to do with the soft muted cloths worn as camouflage by Highland men in the 13th century. The garment is also a 19th century invention— a highly pleated full skirt belted and pinned at the side and worn with a short jacket and white shirt. The modern sporran is also an invention— designed to replace the Highlander's animal skin bag worn at the waist.

The Scottish Tartans Society (STS), which was formed in 1963, studies tartans and keeps a register of all publicly known tartans. More than 2,500 patterns have been listed in the register, which include clan and family tartans, royal tartans, state tartans from the United States, military tartans, and corporate tartans. The two largest tartan groups are the Black Watch and Royal Stewart.

A tartan shop caters mainly to tourists who eagerly purchase all kinds of tartan merchandize— tea-towels, pencils, post-cards, and umbrellas.

LIFESTYLE

SCOTLAND IS CULTURALLY DISTINCT from its southern neighbor England in many ways. England has become a multicultural society with visible ethnic minorities, while Scotland has remained racially homogeneous due to its geographical location and traditions. England has become a largely atheist society, where most people come in contact with the church only at weddings, christenings, and funerals. Scotland, on the other hand, has retained a stronger religious tradition. About 10% of the Scots attend church regularly, compared to 2% in England and Wales.

In England today many people have little sense of a cultural heritage, while Scottish traditions such as music and costume are strong. In other ways Scotland is much like its western European neighbors. Most people live in urban environments, watch television and Hollywood movies, surf the Internet, and enjoy sports. Young people party and listen to the same music as their southern neighbors.

Left: **Schoolgirls wishing each other luck before a performance. Like young people everywhere, teenagers prefer to spend time with their friends than to stay at home.**

Opposite: **A traditional black house or *tigh dubh* ("TICHE DERBF"). These houses are now almost nonexistent, except as museums. The name comes from the smoke (from an indoor peat fire) that is trapped in the upper section of the house.**

Good friends enjoying a drink at a pub. In most pubs a bell will be rung 15 minutes before closing to indicate last orders.

CITY LIFE

Life in the Scottish cities centers on thousands of pubs, designed in different styles to suit different customers. There are Victorian and Edwardian pubs for the older crowd, with quiet corners, peat fires, traditional music, lively games of darts, pub quizzes, and card games. For younger people there are modern designer pubs, sports bars with huge screens showing soccer matches, clubs, and raves, just like their English counterparts.

Most people are away from home during the day, but families usually come together in the evening to share a meal. On weekday evenings most families watch television, although young people often incorporate a late-evening visit to the local pub. Other social activities include going to movies or to the theater, and playing bingo. On weekends most people catch up with the business of running their homes, doing the shopping, taking children to social activities, attending church, or visiting their immediate families.

Prior to the 1990s shops kept very restricted hours, usually office hours, and were closed for half a day once a week. It is now possible to shop late in the evenings and on Sundays. Pubs also have longer opening hours.

Homes tend to be owner-occupied, although there are large areas of housing owned by the government. Row houses are common, with a tiny front yard and larger back garden. In older buildings the toilet was located in the garden. Wealthier people own semidetached houses with three bedrooms, a small kitchen, two downstairs rooms, a garden, and perhaps a garage. Apartment living has become very fashionable in cities where old warehouses have been converted into modern open-plan apartments with shared leisure facilities such as a gym or a pool.

The number of single person homes is on the increase in Scotland as elderly people are left alone after the death of their spouse and younger people choose to live single lives. Two children is typical of the nuclear family; large families tend to be frowned on. The nuclear family is the typical unit, and grandparents usually live separately.

LIFE ON A CROFT

Most crofts are in the Highlands or on the Scottish islands. Until 50 years ago the croft house was known as a *tigh dubh*, or "black house." It was a one-storey building with thick stone walls, about 6 feet (1.8 m) high. The corners of the black house were rounded, and the roof was thatched and held down by ropes weighted with stones. Inside the single room was simple wooden furniture and an open hearth in the center where the cooking was done. Fish-oil lamps were used to light up the house.

These houses have all been replaced in modern times, but some of them still stand and are used as sheds or outhouses. Most modern crofts have solid-fuel stoves, or electricity and running water. They are also equipped with modern furniture and appliances such as refrigerators and washing machines.

The isolation of the crofts means that crofters see little of their neighbors, and shopping or watching a movie means a long trip into town, either by car or boat. Daily work consists of milking cows or tending sheep. Part of the day will be spent on salmon farming, fishing, or road works—whatever job the crofter has taken on to supplement his farm income.

EDUCATION

Most children start school at age 5, although there are some state nursery schools where children attend from age 3. Not all children are guaranteed a place in a state nursery and priority is given to working mothers, often those employed by the state. The state nursery school system is supplemented by private nurseries and playgroups.

From age 5 to 12 children attend primary school where at intervals they take state tests known as SATs. Secondary education lasts until age 16 when students take the Scottish General Certificate of Secondary Education (GCSE) in eight or more subjects. After secondary school, education is by choice, but increasing numbers of students continue to study or take up vocational courses. Scotland has fewer "public," that is privately owned, schools than England. Its most famous, Gordonstone, was attended by Prince Charles, heir to the British throne.

Scotland has eight universities. The oldest are St. Andrews, Glasgow, and Aberdeen—all founded in the 15th century— and Edinburgh, which was established in the 16th century. The newest is the University of Stirling, which opened its doors in 1967. A degree from a Scottish university is different from an English or American one. The program often lasts four years and awards the degree of Master of Arts or Science rather than Bachelor of Arts or Science.

A school excursion breaks the monotony of studying in classrooms and helps to reinforce lessons in a practical manner.

LIFE'S BIG EVENTS

Life's big events—birth, coming-of-age, marriage, and death—are observed in Scotland through the religion and customs of its people. But the ceremonies and traditions associated with these events have decreased in modern Scotland.

BIRTH Traditionally, Scotland treated children born out of wedlock differently than the rest of Britain. In Britain such a child was unable to inherit its father's estate, even if the parents subsequently married. In Scotland, however, marriage legitimized any children of the union. In the past this brought about an unusual custom in the south

A woman reverend relating biblical stories to young children in a Sunday school.

of Scotland, called the hinding system. An agricultural worker was paid more if he brought his wife and children along to work as he could produce more with the assistance of his family. This resulted in a situation where unmarried men had to hire young girls in order to earn their full wages. The men often made the girls pregnant to prove that they were fertile. There was no stigma attached to such a pregnancy.

In modern times women usually give birth in the local maternity hospital, or with the help of a trained midwife if the family lives a long way from town. With the first child they spend a week in the hospital, longer if there are complications. For subsequent childbirths, the stay is usually shorter, sometimes just overnight.

If the child's family follows Christian customs, there will be a christening when the child is formally accepted into the church and given its name. Godparents chosen by the parents promise to look after the spiritual well-being of the child. The child will be dressed for the occasion in an elaborate christening gown. After the ceremony there is often a family party. At these events it is customary to give the baby a gift made of silver.

Some ancient customs associated with childbirth are the groaning cheese and groaning cake—special foods prepared for the mother during her confinement. They are also given after the birth to young girls so that they have easy an delivery in the future. Another superstition is that the cradle and baby buggy must be paid for in advance so the unborn child will not grow up poor. But these items must not be brought in the house before the baby's arrival. A very old Scottish practice was to plunge the newborn baby in cold water to make sure that it would live.

Some parents have no qualms about leaving their babies outside the village store while they run errands.

COMING-OF-AGE This event is celebrated in church at age 13 when children are confirmed in the church. This is often an occasion for a family party. But this ceremony is a rare event today, even among people who are practicing Christians.

Coming-of-age is also celebrated at age 18 when the teenager is legally an adult and eligible to vote, or at 21, which is the traditional age at which young people are considered adults. Whether celebrated at 18 or 21, coming-of-age involves a family party, lots of cards and presents, and in the case of many teenagers, a visit to the pub to celebrate being old enough to drink.

Young people taking photographs to remember a special outing.

WEDDINGS Marriages are less common in Scotland now than in previous times, but when a couple does get married, it is usually in a church. Weddings can also be performed in a registry office or at any other place of one's choice, as long as the ceremony is officiated by a minister. Gretna Green, located near the Scottish-English border, was for many years a place for runaway English couples to marry.

Weddings in Scotland are generally a big family affair. A service takes place in the family's place of worship and is followed by a reception at a local hotel for a large number of guests. Many people hire a horse-drawn carriage or old fashioned cars to get around. The bride wears a white dress and the groom a formal suit or a traditional outfit. The bride may be attended to by bridesmaids, and a best man helps the groom in his part of the ceremony.

GRETNA GREEN

Scotland and England once had different laws regarding the eligibility for marriage. In Scotland a marriage was considered legal if it was declared in front of two witnesses. Thus, from 1774 it became a custom for young English couples who did not have parental consent to go to Scotland to get married. As Gretna Green is the first village over the Scottish border, many weddings were performed there. Due to the quirks of Scottish law, almost anyone could conduct the marriage ceremony. Most couples were married by the village blacksmith, but other residents also performed a fair share of the services.

In the early 20th century, Gretna Green was still a place for quick weddings, since there was no residency requirement in Scotland, and until 1940 a marriage by declaration was still legal in the country. In the 1970s Scottish and English marriage laws were brought into line, so now there is no need to go to Gretna Green. But many people still do so for romantic reasons. The flourishing marriage industry boosts the economy of this small rural village, with hotels catering to families, pipers waiting to play wedding songs in the registry office, and many photographers taking pictures by the Old Blacksmith's Forge.

DEATH When a death occurs even people who have little contact with the church will attend a service for the deceased. In Scotland, as in the rest of Britain, the old tradition of keeping the deceased's body in the house for the wake is no longer practiced. Instead, a funeral director takes responsibility for the entire process: arranging the church service, the funeral paraphernalia, and funeral procession.

Funerals in modern times are expensive, but not as elaborate as they were among wealthy Victorians who built huge monuments to their dead. One surviving example of this is the necropolis in Glasgow, which contains 3,500 tombs and many more graves of modest sizes. The tombs have been a major tourist attraction for over 100 years.

In the city of the dead in Glasgow, the tombs are great towers of limestone and granite, and are of different styles—Roman, Gothic, and even Egyptian.

RELIGION

THE MAIN RELIGION in Scotland is Christianity with several flourishing Christian denominations. The official church is the Church of Scotland, but there are a few Presbyterian sects that separated from the main church during the 19th century over issues of dogma or ritual. The Methodist and Catholic churches are also present. Catholics are chiefly descendants of the Irish immigrants who arrived during the 19th century. In much smaller numbers are Jews, Muslims, Hindus, and Buddhists, all of whom practice their religions freely in Scottish cities. In Glasgow there are many synagogues, mosques, and a Buddhist center.

Evidence of religion in Scotland dates back well before the arrival of Christianity and can be seen in the many standing stones and burial grounds of prehistoric times. Some aspects of these early religions lingered in Scotland well into Christian times. Scotland's long history of superstition and belief in witchcraft may be the remnants of these earlier religions.

Left: **This chapel was constructed during World War II by Italian prisoners of war in Orkney. It was restored in 1960.**

Opposite: **A boy in deep thought after attending church.**

THE EARLY CHRISTIANS

Christianity first came to Scotland in the time of the Romans. The first Christian church is said to have been set up by St. Ninian in Whithorn, near the Solway Firth, at around A.D. 400. However, Christianity made little impression on the inhabitants of Scotland until the sixth century, when Irish missionaries, led by St. Columba arrived and set up a monastery on Iona Island in the Inner Hebrides. St. Columba's ability to speak Gaelic helped him convert many to the Celtic church, among them the Picts and Scots. As a result, many of the warring tribes in Scotland became united by a common religion.

The Christianity practiced by St. Columba was slightly different from that in the rest of Europe, with abbots superior to bishops and Easter set at a different date. In the Middle Ages, Christianity in Scotland was brought in line with the rest of Europe. Scotland was divided into 11 bishoprics whose bishops wielded political power and determined religious policies. Clerics were celibate in keeping with the beliefs of the church.

THE REFORMATION

The Reformation, led by intellectuals such as John Calvin and Martin Luther, took place across 16th century Europe. They broke away from the Roman Catholic Church, which had become very corrupt and was more concerned with power than with the spiritual needs of the congregation. The Reformers rewrote the Bible in language that their congregations could understand and removed hierarchy in churches.

In Scotland it was Calvin's ideas that took hold. A French philosopher who helped reform the church in Switzerland, Calvin advocated putting the Bible in the forefront of Christian religion as opposed to the word of the bishops. He believed in predestination: that if God is omnipotent or

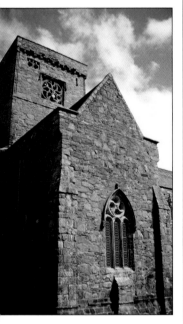

The church tower of Iona Abbey, established by St. Columba in A.D. 563. Iona Abbey attracted many visitors after its restoration in the 1930s. The royal cemetery was the resting place of Scottish kings until the 11th century. Forty-eight sovereigns are said to be buried here, including Duncan, who was murdered by Macbeth in 1040.

all-knowing, he must know what will happen to each person before they are born. This puts enormous pressure on the individual to behave in a godly manner to prove that he or she is one of the Elect, the people predetermined by God to enter the Kingdom of Heaven.

Led by John Knox, the Scottish Reformers established their own church in 1560. But the church was divided on whether to adopt the Presbyterian or Episcopalian form of government, the former preferring a church without state control and a hierarchy without bishops. A century of religious strife ended in 1689 when the Scottish Parliament and courts decreed that the Church of Scotland would be Presbyterian in government.

JOHN KNOX

Born in 1513 in Haddington in the Lothian region, John Knox was a Roman Catholic priest when he was persuaded by Scottish reformer George Wishart to be part of the reformation of the Scottish church. After the archbishop of St. Andrews burned Wishart for heresy, the Reformers holed up in St. Andrews Castle. In 1547 the governor of Scotland, with the help of the French, stormed the castle and arrested the Reformers. Knox was sent into slavery to work on a ship's galley. He was released 19 months later through the intervention of the English. Knox returned to Scotland in 1595 and began to preach.

In 1560 the Church of Scotland was established. Schools were built, and the church grew more powerful every year. John Knox died in 1572. There are memorials and statues erected to him all over Scotland. His influence even extends to the architecture of church buildings. Early churches that were elaborate Gothic creations gave way to simple buildings designed to enable the maximum number of people to listen to the preacher.

THE CHURCH OF SCOTLAND

The Church of Scotland is fiercely democratic and does not have hierarchy or bishops. Lay people as well as ministers run the kirk, or church, and hold church courts known as kirk sessions to determine church policy. But only ordained ministers can administer baptism and communion. Ministers, who can be either male or female, are chosen by the congregation, not appointed by a higher authority, and the leader of the kirk, the moderator, assumes office for only a year. There are 1,200 ordained ministers and 1,292 churches. The churches are generally plain, with little decoration.

The doctrines of the church are moderate, and intellectual deviation is tolerated. In the 19th century the Calvinist belief in predestination was moderated by theologians of the church who proposed that atonement was possible. Through good works and faith, anyone can go to heaven. Beliefs in the literal truth of the Bible were also challenged as scientists discovered that geology did not support the idea of a seven-day creation, and Darwin's theories suggested that man had evolved, not been created.

Today the Church of Scotland, like the Church of England, has adapted its ideas to suit modern knowledge. A firmly held belief in the real existence of hell and the predetermined place of most human beings in it has given way to a belief that hell is simply a state of mind and that everyone can be redeemed.

THE FREE CHURCH OF SCOTLAND

Early in the 18th century the Church of Scotland split in two sects: the Moderates, who were mainly concerned with social matters and cultural activities, and the Evangelicals, who adhered strictly to Calvinist beliefs. In the 19th century the Evangelicals wanted the church to be independent of the state and the congregation to choose their minister, not the landowners who were patrons of the church. When their demands were rejected, the Evangelicals decided to leave the church. At a General Assembly of the Church of Scotland on May 18, 1843, two-fifths of the clergy walked out and formed a new church.

The Free Church of Scotland was very popular in the late 19th century. It enforced strict adherence to the rules regarding the Sabbath, or Sunday, and expected its members to attend services twice a day. In 1847 the Free Church joined the United Presbyterian Church, which had also broken away from the Church of Scotland. The main body of the Free Church reunited with the Church of Scotland in 1929 when it became independent of the state. Those who were against the union continued as the Free Church of Scotland.

Today there are areas in Scotland where the Free Church dominates—the Outer Hebrides on Harris, North Uist, and Lewis Islands. On the Sabbath the islanders wear dark clothes, do no work, not even cooking, and any washing left over from the previous day must be brought inside. Fishing boats must be at anchor. Until recently few ferries ran to the islands on Sundays.

In the early 1990s a new school was built on Benbecula Island to serve the Catholic southern islands and the Free Church northern islands. The council, dominated by Free Churchers, refused to appoint supervisory staff for the Sabbath and caused an uproar among the Catholic community who wanted to use the school's leisure facilities on Sundays.

Opposite: **The interior of Rosslyn Chapel located in Roslin, a village about 6 miles (10 km) south of Edinburgh. Built in 1446, the chapel is said to have the most green man—vegetation emerging from the mouth of a male head—images of any medieval building in Scotland. The green man symbolizes renewal and rebirth.**

Meditations are a part of a Buddhist's daily ritual.

ROMAN CATHOLICISM

Roman Catholicism was the pre-Reformation religion of Scotland and was seen by most Scots as the religion of Scotland's oppressors. In the 18th century about 20,000 people, chiefly in remote rural areas, were still Roman Catholic. This changed radically in the 19th century with the influx of refugees from Ireland to Scottish cities. By 1951 there were about 750,000 Roman Catholics in Scotland, mainly of Irish descent. Catholicism is strongest in urban areas where the Irish first settled, but there is also a strong tradition of Catholicism in Aberdeenshire, in the eastern Highlands, and the southern Hebrides, on South Uist, Eriskay, and Barra Islands.

OTHER RELIGIONS

Scotland has many other religious groups—either sects of the Church of Scotland or other religions. The Episcopalian Church is strong among the upper classes of Scotland. It is the equivalent of the Church of England and observes ornate rituals compared with the Presbyterian churches. The Free

Presbyterian Church, a radical sect that still flourishes in Scotland, believe the Pope to be the Antichrist and Roman Catholic Mass to be a blasphemy. There are also Baptist churches and several Evangelical groups, as well as communities of Jews, Hindus, and Muslims.

SUPERSTITIONS AND SORCERY

In the 17th century people though to be witches were tied up and thrown in deep water. If they floated, they were guilty of practicing witchcraft. In Scotland, someone found guilty of witchcraft was tied to a stake and strangled. This was known as wirrying. Afterwards, the body was burned. Witchcraft laws were abandoned in 1735.

Other beliefs, probably inherited from ancient religions, center on lakes and wells and have continued to the present day. Clootie wells are thought to have curative powers over certain diseases. A particular well at Culloden is visited by busloads of people on May day, and money is thrown into the well as a petition for the well being of the visitors. At other wells pieces of cloth are hung on the branches of nearby trees. The pieces belong to sick people who hope that by hanging up something belonging to them they may be cured.

Another ancient tradition in Scotland is that of *taibhsearachd* (THAIBF-seer-a-chad), or "second sight." One famous 17th century seer, Còinneach Odhar, saw the future by looking through a stone with a hole through it. He prophesied the depopulation of the Highlands, the end of crofting, and the construction of the Caledonian canal. The most uncanny of his prophecies concerned the Ness River: when it was possible to walk dryshod across the river in five places, a terrible disaster would befall the world. The fifth bridge over the Ness River opened in August 1939. On September 1 Germany invaded Poland and World War II began.

Underpopulated areas like Scotland seem to attract communities of people who seek to get away from civilization. One of these is the Findhorn Foundation that was set up in 1962 in northeast Scotland. Two hundred people now live there permanently, and around 8,000 visitors arrive each year. The settlement is established along sound ecological lines, using natural sewage treatment, solar energy, and earthern roofs.

LANGUAGE

THE DOMINANT LANGUAGE of Scotland today is English, but that is a recent development. The early inhabitants, the Picts, spoke a language that is little known—except that place names beginning with "pit" probably evolved from this pre-Roman language. Another language spoken in southern Scotland by an early tribe, the Britons, was British, which is thought to resemble Welsh. The word *caer*, meaning fort, that appears in some place names is a survival of the British language.

Much later, long after Gaelic became the dominant language of Scotland, another language entered the melting pot—the Norse language, spoken by the Viking settlers of the Orkney and Shetland Islands. In parts of Shetland a language called Norn, which is descended from the Vikings' language, was spoken until the 18th century. The influence of Norn can still be seen in place names that contain the words *bister*, meaning farmstead, *by*, or village, and *wick*, meaning bay.

Left: **Street musicians thank tourists in four languages for donations.**

Opposite: **A newsstand is packed with local and foreign periodicals and newspapers.**

GAELIC

Gaelic arrived in Scotland with the Scots sometime in the fifth century. As the tribes spread across the country, and Scots monks led by St. Columba on Iona became an important influence with the Pictish chiefs, Gaelic became the lingua franca, or the language used by speakers of different languages to communicate. By the 10th century Gaelic had become the native tongue in most of Scotland. By the 13th century, 800 years after the language had arrived in Scotland, it had become a dialect separate from Irish Gaelic and was spoken throughout Scotland, except on the Shetland and Orkney islands.

After the 13th century, as English and French influence spread across Scotland and wealth and land systematically began to be transferred into English hands, Gaelic began to be replaced by the language of the Normans. The Celtic church of St. Columba was converted to the Church of Rome, and the language of the bishops was either English or French. As trade increased, English merchants settled in the towns. That was another incentive to speak English.

The Jacobite rebellions and Highland clearances in the 18th and 19th centuries speeded the decline of Gaelic. In 1872 the Education Act eliminated Gaelic in Scottish schools. Children were punished for speaking the language in the classroom. Today about 250,000 people have some knowledge of Gaelic, with around 86,000 in the northwest Highlands and Hebrides speaking it fluently. This number is on the increase since provision has been made in the last decade for Gaelic classes in schools and there are some bilingual primary schools. On the Isle of Skye, there is even a Gaelic college, Sabhal Mòr Ostaig. In addition, there has been an enormous increase in the number of Gaelic-language television and radio programs, and publishing in Gaelic is flourishing.

Gaelic belongs to the Celtic group of the Indo-European language family, which also includes Irish and Welsh. Although Gaelic has only 18 letters, it is a highly complex language and is difficult to master.

Below: **The Isle of Skye is home to the largest number of Gaelic speakers in Scotland. About 60% of the population still uses the language in everyday life.**

Opposite: **The name of a shop in both English and Gaelic.**

SCOTS

Scots is only used in Scotland; it is not spoken anywhere else in the world. There is no standard spoken or written form of the language. Each region where Scots is used has its own dialect.

Scots, or Lowland Scottish, or Lallan, used to be widely spoken in southern and eastern Scotland. Now Scots is only spoken in northeast Scotland. Scots comes from Northern English, which gradually replaced Gaelic as the lingua franca from the 11th to 14th centuries. In the early 1300s Northern English was spoken by people living in the eastern and southern

AN EXCERPT OF *TO A MOUSE, ON TURNING HER UP IN HER NEST WITH THE PLOUGH* BY ROBERT BURNS

Wee, sleeket, cowran, tim'rous beastie,
O what panic's in thy breastie!
Thou need na start awa sae hasty,
Wi' bickering brattle!
I wad be laith to rin an' chase thee,
Wi' murd'ring pattle!

I'm truly sorry Man's dominion
Has broken Nature's social union,
An' justifies that ill opinion
Which makes thee startle,
At me, thy poor, earth-born companion,
An' fellow-mortal!

I doubt na, whyles, but thou may thieve;
What then? poor beastie, thou maun live!
A daimen-icker in a thrave
'S a sma' request:
I'll get a blessin wi' the lave,
An' never miss't!

Highlands. By 1328 this language was known as Scots. It was also the language that writers and intellectuals used. By 1424 Scots had replaced Latin as the official language of government. In the 14th to 16th centuries, a literary Scots language had developed.

Scots and Northern English drifted apart in the 15th and 16th centuries. But in the mid-1500s the language of the Scots became more anglicanized as the power of England increased. During the Reformation, English was used as the language of the bible. By the 18th century Scots was regarded as the language of the common people. Today Scots is only considered a regional dialect.

The grammar of Scots is very similar to English, but the spelling is different. There are many words that are not present in English. Examples of these are *dreich* ("TREECH"), meaning dull, *daundring* ("DORN-dring"), or walking slowly, and *roup* ("ROOP"), meaning auction. In addition Scots retains some words that were once part of the English language but have since disappeared. In Scots the plural of the word shoe is *sheen*, while the plural of eye is *een*.

The most famous writer in the Scots language is the poet Robert Burns (1759-1796), who collected old folk tales and songs and rewrote them in his own style. A modern writer using Scots is the poet Hugh McDiarmid.

Scotland's national poet, Robert Burns (1759–1796) wrote over 300 poems and songs.

SCOTTISH ENGLISH

Any English-speaking person who visits Scotland will have no difficulty in understanding what is said after the initial difficulties of accents and usage are overcome. In Britain an event called the great vowel shift took place during medieval times. Anyone who has read Geoffrey Chaucer's work will recognize that English has changed enormously over the centuries. Chaucer's English predates the vowel shift and is closer to the Scottish English spoken in some parts of Scotland, where the shift did not occur. Thus you might hear a Scot saying *tak* instead of the English "take," or *bool* instead of the English "bowl."

In addition English usage has changed or been influenced by Scots or Gaelic over the years so that when English people say "I doubt you'll need an umbrella," they mean that it is not going to rain. But when Scottish people say the same words, they mean that it will rain! They use the expression "I doubt that" to mean "I'm sorry to say that." To an Englishman "doing the messages" means sending e-mail to people. To a Scot it means shopping for groceries. To a Scot, "I'll see you the length of the bus stop" means he'll walk you to the bus stop. To an Englishman it means nothing at all.

Scots has a number of idiomatic expressions. Some are "a bald head is easily shaved" (an easy job is soon finished), "a closed mouth catches no flies" (a person who keeps silent causes no trouble), "a green turf is a good mother-in-law" (the best mother-in-law to have is a dead one), "a scabby sheep often infects a flock" (one bad person can hurt the whole community), and "a horn spoon holds no poison" (eating in a poor person's house is not dangerous). In the old days only poor people used spoons made of horn. In rich houses where there were metal spoons, there would be intrigue over money, and people were liable to get poisoned.

OGHAM WRITING

Ogham ("O-hum") writing is a form of writing used by the Celts. A few examples exist in Scotland, but it is much more common to find examples of this early writing in Ireland and on the Isle of Man. Some examples of Ogham writing have been found on Pictish monuments, which are more commonly decorated with pictures. Ogham writing was used until the 10th century when it was replaced by the writing brought by St. Columba from Ireland.

The writing consists of a series of strokes made across the corner of a piece of stone. The strokes correspond to 19 of the characters of the English alphabet and a character representing the "ng" sound. The vowels are cut across the corner of the stone, while the consonants are represented by a series of diagonals or incisions to the right or left of the corner.

The most famous Ogham stone in Scotland is at Dunadd in Argyll (western Scotland), which is thought to be a very ancient coronation spot for the Gaelic kings. At Bandsbutt in Inverurie is an ancient stone monument that contains both Ogham writing and Pictish symbols.

An Ogham stone at Newton in Aberdeenshire, eastern Scotland.

Children totally engrossed in front of the television set.

TELEVISION

Scotland is served by five terrestrial television channels and 10 satellite channels. The terrestrial channels include the two national television stations, BBC 1 and 2, which offer high quality productions of costume dramas, modern plays, comedy shows, and serious documentaries. Of the three national commercial channels, Channel 4 offers an alternative, slightly highbrow schedule, while Grampian and Border are Scottish-based commercial channels. The most recent national commercial channel, called Channel 5, is lowbrow and offers docu-soaps, which are long-running documentaries on people in the community. Channel 5 also offers movies and what is known as "dumbed down" news reporting, or simplified news bulletins.

Satellite television is dominated by the BSkyB network, with a series of channels dedicated to movies, comedy shows, nature programs, sports, and other interests. The Sky channels rarely produce their own material, concentrating on reruns of BBC or ITV (Independent Television) programs, or American imports.

NEWPAPERS

Scotland enjoys special editions of British newspapers aimed at Scottish interests. The national newspapers are divided into two categories—tabloid and broadsheet. Broadsheet technically refers to the size of the newspaper, but in actual fact, it has more to do with the quality of the news reporting, which is better than that of the tabloids.

There are three tabloids—*Daily Mirror*, a vaguely socialist newspaper with lots of gossip and little real news; *The Sun*, which for many years combined right-wing politics with semi-naked women on page three, the "Page Three Girls;" and *Daily Sport*, which concentrates on sex-related gossip.

The four broadsheets have political allegiances. *The Times* and *Telegraph* are both traditionally right-wing, although *The Times* has moved to the political center. Of the other two broadsheets, *The Guardian* has left-wing leanings, while *The Independent* adopts a neutral tone in its reporting.

There are three Scottish daily papers—*The Scotsman*, published in Edinburgh, is mildly liberal; Glasgow's center-right *The Herald*; and a tabloid called the *Daily Record*. There are many provincial papers, all of which are widely read. Most of the national papers have a Sunday version with special Scottish editions. There is also a Scottish broadsheet called *Scotland on Sunday*, and a tabloid called *Sunday Post*, that is read by at least half of the Scottish population.

A newsstand selling a variety of newspapers in different languages.

ARTS

BESIDES PRODUCING MORE THAN its share of the world's scientists and inventors, Scotland has also contributed to the world's culture in no small measure. Scottish music, which has a long tradition, flourishes today, either in its original form or as contemporary music. Scottish painting, which did not exist until the 18th century, now boasts several outstanding artists such as the Glasgow Boys and Charles Rennie Mackintosh who fused art and architecture. Famous literary works range from the powerful writings of Sir Walter Scott and Robert Burns to novelist John Buchan and playwright James Barrie. The Scottish movie industry, though small, produces internationally acclaimed work.

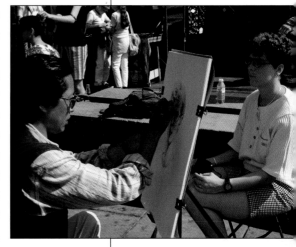

Above: **A tourist getting her portrait drawn.**

Opposite: **A pavement artist's eye-catching work decorates Princes Street in Edinburgh.**

SHETLAND MUSIC

The Shetland Islands have a long tradition of fiddle playing in a distinctive style. Like other Scottish traditions, this came very close to extinction in the 1970s, when young people on the islands migrated to the cities in search of better work opportunities, and the music was not passed along to this generation. But Shetland music, like other types of Scottish music, has undergone a revival in recent times, thanks to performers who tirelessly promote it.

The most famous proponent of Shetland music is Aly Bain, who is also a novelist and television presenter. Together with two Irishmen and another Scot, Mike Whelan, he formed a band called Boys of the Lough, which has enjoyed success for 25 years. This has encouraged young Shetlanders to take up the fiddle. In the 21st century Shetland music has a strong and vibrant future.

TRADITIONAL MUSIC

Traditional Scottish music, played on acoustic guitar, bagpipes, accordion, and fiddle, is less popular than its Irish cousin. Like Irish music, Scottish music, in the 1960s, was mistakenly thought to consist of sentimental ballads played by an orchestra and sung by a man wearing a sweater.

This image was due to a popular 1960s British television show called The White Heather Club. Singers dressed in tartan would sing sad or comic songs, and the program often included displays of Highland dancing and lone bagpipers playing morose-sounding tunes. As a result, young people were uninterested in traditional Scottish music.

At the same time folk music in Scotland was popularized through the influence of Bob Dylan. Traditional musicians thus turned to folk music as a medium of expression. Bands that achieved fame included The Incredible String Band, Pentangle, and Jethro Tull, but their music sounded more like folk music than traditional Scottish music.

It was not until the late 1970s that Scottish traditional music really came back in fashion with bands like Boys of the Lough and Battlefield Band, who tried to breathe new life into Scottish music. Later, bands incorporated bagpipes in contemporary rock music, something which would have been unthinkable 10 years earlier. By the 1980s popular British bands such as Capercaillie, Runrig, Seelyhoo, and Shooglenifty had successfully merged contemporary rock and traditional Scottish music.

THE BAGPIPES

Although the bagpipes are strongly associated with Scotland, they are not exclusively a Scottish instrument. They were said to have originated in the near East, and there are versions of the pipes throughout Europe, and even in India and Russia. Bagpipes are thought to have appeared in Scotland in the 15th century. In Scotland there are two types of bagpipes—Lowland or Border bagpipes that are blown by a bellows held under the piper's arm; and Highland bagpipes, which are blown using the mouth.

Highland bagpipes are most commonly played. They consist of a bag that is inflated by blowing into a leather blowpipe. The bag is held under one arm. By squeezing the bag, the player can control the amount of air that flows through the other pipes—three drone and a chanter—that have double reeds. The piper plays tunes on the chanter, which has eight finger holes and points down.

Highland bagpipes were created by clan pipers as an instrument for military bands. They are designed to be played outdoors, while the Lowlands bagpipes are indoor instruments. Piping tunes were often written to commemorate important events in Scottish history and are often sad sounding pieces.

The music of the Highland pipes, or *pibroch* ("PHIT-roch"), is divided into two types—marches in different tempos and tunes based on a theme followed by up to 10 variations. The music is often played solo and must be listened to in silence. Lowland pipes often accompany social events such as dances and have been incorporated into modern Scottish rock music.

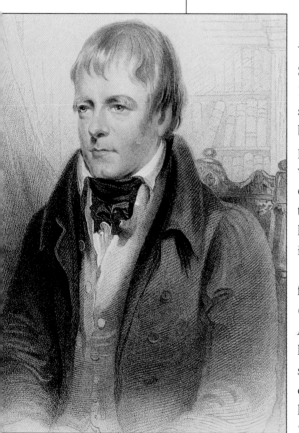

A portrait of Sir Walter Scott, novelist, poet, biographer, and historian.

FAMOUS LITERARY FIGURES

Scotland's most famous writer is Sir Walter Scott (1771–1832). Scott became interested in traditional Scottish stories and ballads as a child and when he grew up, he began collecting and rewriting old ballads. In 1802 he published the songs he had collected and as the book was extremely popular, he became famous almost overnight. Unfortunately he spent more money than his two jobs (deputy sheriff and Court of Session clerk) and his income from writing provided and so fell hopelessly in debt.

Scott drew on his knowledge of Scottish history and folklore to publish many historical novels, particularly *Old Mortality* (1816), *Rob Roy* (1818), and *The Heart of Midlothian*. Having used all the Scottish folk stories he knew, he turned to English tales and had enormous success with the novel *Ivanhoe* (1819). To finish paying off his enormous debts, Scott worked very hard, and his health worsened. He died at the age of 39. By the mid-20th century Scott's novels had become unfashionable, but there was a revival of interest after the movie *Rob Roy* appeared in 1995, and several television productions were adapted from his works.

Robert Burns (1759–1796), the national poet of Scotland, wrote in his native language. His work sentimentalizes ordinary people and satirizes the church and state. Burns was born to a large family. His father, a tenant farmer, died penniless and in debt. Thus the young poet resented the politicians and rich landlords.

When Burns became head of the family, he found a farm to live on. In his free time he wrote poetry for his own amusement and to entertain his friends. Burns, like his father, did not have much success as a tenant farmer and wanted to leave Scotland. Before he did, he published his poetry. *Poems Chiefly in the Scottish Dialect* (1786) became popular, enjoyed by both the intellectuals in Edinburgh and ordinary people. Burns moved to Edinburgh, but left after a while because he was unhappy there.

He later found a job collecting and rewriting traditional Scottish ballads, producing songs such as "Auld Lang Syne," "Comin' Through the Rye," and "Green Grow the Rashes." Burns never received any payment for his work as he saw what he was doing as a way of contributing to his country. He died in Dumfriesshire at age 37 of rheumatic heart disease.

Robert Burns' birthday, on January 25, is celebrated in Scotland as well as by Scots living overseas.

A memorial to Robert Burns in his birthplace, Alloway.

A battle scene in the movie *Braveheart*, which is about the life of Scottish hero Sir William Wallace. An irony about the movie is that it was not filmed in Scotland. Most of the battles were filmed in Ireland where the film makers had more cooperation from the government. Most of the Scotsmen in the battle scenes are actually members of the Irish Territorial Army.

THE MOVIE INDUSTRY

Two films in modern times seem to sum up the different faces of Scotland. *Braveheart* conjures up a romantic image of a strong but downtrodden nation fighting for its soul and independence. In *Trainspotting*, heroin addicts eke out a degraded existence, and one of them berates Scotland for being ruled by effete and useless people.

Scotland does not get European Union funding for its small industries. So the Scottish film industry is underfunded and very small. But Scotland has assisted foreign film companies looking for movie locations. In 1999 several big American productions were filmed in Scotland: *K19*, a movie about the Cold War, was filmed in Rosyth Dock, while Glasgow's old buildings were used to represent turn-of-the-century New York in *The House of Mirth*, starring Gillian Anderson. The blockbuster movie *Entrapment*, starring Sean Connery and Catherine Zeta Jones, was also filmed in Scotland. These foreign productions provide much needed funds for Scotland's own film industry.

ARCHITECTURE

Long after the wealthy in England gave up fortifying their grand houses, castle building in Scotland continued as the country was still filled with unrest well into the 17th century. The typical Scottish castle is in fact a fortified tower house built for defense as well as accommodation. Their defensive nature shows in the bare ground floor; windows and decoration only appear above ground level so that attackers do not have easy access.

After the 17th century more and more living quarters were added until the tower houses began to resemble fairy-tale castles, which the Scottish tourist board now uses in advertisements. Glamis Castle is a typical castle of this sort with plenty of ornamental turrets and other embellishments on the top floors but plain walls with no windows below. Castles built in the 18th and even 19th century had all the grand scale of older castles, but the defensive element of their design was gone. Big ground floor windows, huge entrance staircases, massive doors, and many entrances were more typical design features.

Glamis Castle, the setting of William Shakespeare's play *Macbeth*.

TENEMENTS

During the Industrial Revolution, masses of people from the Highlands and Islands moved to the cities in search of work, and tenements were built to house them. Most tenements were built by private landlords between 1860 and the early 20th century.

The early structures consist of rows of three-storey buildings, often constructed back to back so that little light or air penetrated the interior. Even though the tenements were built to accommodate a lot of people, they soon grew overcrowded, even more so than the designers had anticipated. The buildings later came under the control of city planners, who insisted that the tenements be built using designs that would provide a healthier environment.

In Glasgow 21,052 tenement houses were built between 1872 and 1876. Little thought was given to their outward appearance, and the decoration consisted largely of variations in the window design, with plain windows broken up by occasional bays. In the 20th century many of these buildings were torn down to be replaced by high-rise apartments.

A larger than life mural on the wall of a tenement building.

In modern times the tenements in the inner cities have become fashionable. Renovated and redecorated, they provide housing for much smaller families than once lived in them. In the Garnethill area of Glasgow, one row of superior tenements, those once lived in by skilled workers or perhaps clerical workers, has been acquired by the National Trust, and one of the apartments has been restored to its original condition.

SCOTTISH ARTISTS

The man who bridged the gap between art and architecture was Charles Rennie Mackintosh (1868–1928). As a child he painted the countryside where he lived, and as a teenager he attended the Glasgow School of Art. His design ideas fused Art Nouveau with influences from Japanese art and the artist Aubrey Beardsley. In 1896 he won the competition to design the new Glasgow School of Art building, and this is today his greatest work. He also designed interiors of buildings, and it is in this area that Mackintosh is most famous today, with his designs for crockery, interior decoration, and furniture. He retired to Suffolk, and later to France, where he concentrated on drawing. Mackintosh was dismissed as an eccentric in Scotland, but his work gained recognition in Europe. It is only in the last 30 years that his talent has been acknowledged in Scotland.

In the 1880s a group of young men studying in the Edinburgh Royal Scottish Academy became known as the Glasgow Boys. They were strongly influenced by the French Impressionists and painted rural scenes as well as scenes of street life in the city. They rejected the traditional Scottish style of historical and allegorical scenes painted in a romantic fashion as unreal and sentimental. The chief proponents of the Glasgow Boys' style were James (later Sir) Guthrie, John (later Sir) Lavery, George Henry and E. A. Hornel. The Glasgow Boys had a major effect on Scottish art, altering it forever and giving it new life.

A relief map of the city of Edinburgh greets visitors at the entrance of the National Gallery of Scotland.

97

LEISURE

THE SCOTS ENJOY a wide range of activities in their leisure time, from traditional Scottish Highland games to the British national game of soccer. Other popular sports include skiing, fishing, and golf, which was invented in Scotland.

For the less active, watching television, going to the movies, and playing or listening to music are the preferred leisure activities. The cities have casinos, theaters, movie houses, concert halls, and art galleries to occupy a Scot's leisure time. Some Scots like to go pub crawling.

Like other British people, many Scots have gardens, and gardening has become a big business leisure industry in the last decade, with people spending as much on plants and garden furnishings as they do on decorating the inside of their homes.

Below: **A family kayaking.**

Opposite: **Participants in a Highland dancing competition. Girls are most commonly seen in these competition, even though once in a while a young boy is spotted.**

Children are not left out of the fun in the Highland games.

HIGHLAND GAMES

Originally a 14th century method of choosing the strongest fighters among the clan's warriors, Highland games became fashionable in the 19th century when Queen Victoria took an interest in Scottish culture. More a festival than a sport, the games take place throughout the summer.

Tossing the caber is the most spectacular of the Highland games. This involves a strong man lifting an entire tree trunk with its branches removed and running a required distance with it. At the end of the run, he must throw the caber vertically so it makes a neat landing farther along. The distance the caber travels, grace in running, and accuracy of throw determine the winner of the competition.

Another Highland game is putting the stone—similar to shot put, the Olympic field event, but using a lump of rock. A third event is tossing a 56 lb (25 kg) hammer over a bar. Tourism has altered the highland games a lot. They are now geared to visitors and include parachute jumps, visits by minor celebrities, a fair, and exhibitions of dancing and piping.

SOCCER

Soccer is Scotland's national sport. Every Saturday during the autumn and winter and well into the summer, thousands of supporters stream to soccer grounds to stand in cold, damp, and uncomfortable conditions to watch their teams play. Soccer support is tribal in nature and fans spend the entire match singing songs about the superb qualities of their own team, the inadequacies of the opposing team, and the questionable lineage of the referee. At big matches where a lot depends on the outcome, there is occasional violence between supporters of the two teams.

A goalkeeper makes a crucial save, robbing the rival team of a goal.

At the local level, there is the Scottish Football League, which has four divisions. The best clubs play in the Scottish Premier League, which is dominated by two teams, Celtic and Rangers. Based in Glasgow, these teams do not represent areas in Glasgow, but religious groups; Celtic is the Catholic team, and Rangers the Protestant. When these two teams play, there is often violence made more ugly by its sectarian nature. In the 1990s the Glasgow Rangers have dominated the Scottish Premier League, while the Glasgow Celtic have been in second place.

Small though it is, Scotland has produced some of Britain's most memorable soccer players: Dennis Law, Kenny Dalglish, Billy Bremner, and Graham Souness. The country has also produced some of Britain's best soccer managers, including Jock Stein; Sir Matt Busby, who managed the 1996 English World Cup team; Bill Shankly; and Alex Ferguson, who is in charge of England's most successful football team of all time—Manchester United.

GOLF

Tradition claims that golf was invented on the sand dunes of the east coast of Scotland. An early form of golf was played by Mary Queen of Scots, who was said to have played golf shortly after her husband's murder. In Scotland golf is more popular and less expensive and elitist than in the rest of Britain. Scotland has more than 400 golf courses, with more greens per square mile of territory than any other country in the world. Most people play on public golf courses, which are owned by local councils, but there are many private courses, which are more expensive and exclusive. In very remote areas of Scotland, there is no caretaker for the golf course and players using the course are asked to put the greens fee in an honesty box.

St. Andrews golf course is the base of the Royal and Ancient Golf Club, the worldwide governing body of golf that decides the rules of the game. St. Andrews has six courses; the most famous is the Old Course with only 11 instead of 18 greens and two short holes instead of four.

Playing golf at St. Andrews, which has been around since the 15th century. In the background is the St. Andrews Golf Club, the oldest in the world. It was established in 1754.

OTHER SPORTS

Besides being an occupation, fishing in Scotland is also a major leisure pursuit. Scotland has hundreds of miles of inland water ways and an enormous coastline, all perfect places for the keen fisherman. Fishing licenses are seldom necessary, and game fish such as trout and salmon are abundant.

Surfing is also popular in Scotland, which is unusual given its cold climate. Avid surfers head for the north coast, where the waves are comparable to Hawaii at times. Skiing is a fairly recent introduction; there was no local tradition of skiing. There are small ski resorts in the Cairngorms, Glencoe, Glenshee, the Lecht, and Nevis Range, where it is best to ski in February and sometimes March. In the same area the Siberian Husky Club holds annual races.

Curling is another Scottish sport invented about 500 years ago. It is similar to the English game of lawn bowling but is played on ice. Players throw curling stones across the ice at a target. The stones are circular, slightly flat, very heavy, and have a handle. Players are allowed to clear the loose snow in front of the stone as it moves. The player whose stone is nearest the target wins the game.

Skiing is fast becoming a popular activity among young Scots.

FESTIVALS

SCOTLAND IS A LAND OF FESTIVALS, some of them international in outlook and others pagan and local in origin. There are many arts festivals too, the most famous being the Edinburgh International Festival. Big cities are not the only places that celebrate colorful festivals; the smallest villages also have festivals of their own with origins and purposes lost in the mists of time. One way to look at the festivals of Scotland is to describe them as they occur through the year.

HOGMANAY

No one is quite sure of the origin of the Scottish name for New Year's Eve. Theories suggest that it may have come from the Anglo-Saxon *Haleg Monath* ("HAW-lech Mon-arth"), or Holy Month, or the Gaelic *oge maidne* ("AWK MAYD-neh"), meaning new morning. Whatever the origins of the name, Hogmanay is one of the most important festivals in Scotland, outweighing Christmas in significance. Until modern times, gifts were given to children at Hogmanay rather than at Christmas.

An event that takes place in the early hours of New Year's morning is called first footing. Great importance is placed on the nature of the first person to step over the threshold in the New Year. The first choice is for a tall, handsome, dark-haired stranger, although in some areas blonde or red-haired visitors are best. Women may not be first footers because they are deemed to bring bad luck. The first footer must bring gifts—fuel for the fire, bread or salt so that the family will not go hungry, and whisky. If he comes empty-handed, it is seen as a deliberate attempt to harm the family. In another tradition practiced for the good luck of the house, the back door to the house is opened just before midnight to let out the old

Above: **Christmas was not celebrated in Scotland until the mid-1900s. Before then, Christmas Day was business as usual for shops and offices.**

Opposite: **The Edinburgh International Festival attracts performers, both amateurs and professionals, from all over Britain and of all ages.**

The Beltane Fire Festival on the night of April 30 is held in Edinburgh. Known also as May Eve and Walpurgis Night, the festival has its roots in an ancient Celtic ritual that celebrates the arrival of summer.

year. As the new year begins, the front door is opened to let it in. In some regions of Scotland an even more ancient tradition is played out on Hogmanay—burning out the old year. In Comrie there is a torchlit procession led by costumed people who light torches attached to six-foot poles. They parade around the village to the tunes of pipers and then throw the torches down in the middle of the square. Everyone dances around the fire until the embers burn out. In Wick a huge bonfire, built over the previous two months, is lit in a park. In Biggar the bonfire is built big enough to last all night, while revellers toast kippers in the flames.

FIRE FESTIVALS

In January there are more fire-centered ceremonies, all ancient and pagan in nature. In the early hours of January 1 at Stonehaven, residents go through the town whirling fireballs around their heads to drive away evil spirits and welcome the new year. In Burghead, in Moray, on January 11, which was the end of the old year before the calendar changed in 1752, a metal basket is made at a special site by the young men in a particular local family. The basket used to be specially forged for the occasion, but these days a tar barrel or whisky cask is used. The *clavie* ("CLA-vy"), as the basket is called, is filled with tar-soaked wood, and at 6 p.m. it is lit with a piece of peat from a household fire. The men take turns carrying this burning tar barrel on their heads through the town. They must not trip, or mischief will befall the whole village the following year. As they go around the village, the men give smoldering pieces of wood to everyone they pass to bring them luck. Eventually the *clavie* ends up on an ancient mound, where it is smashed to pieces and revellers fight for pieces of lucky wood.

The Up-Helly-Aa festival ends in a blaze of glory.

In January the Shetland Islands have fire festivals. The biggest, at Lerwick on the last Tuesday in January, is known as Up-Helly-Aa. This marks the end of the Viking festival of Yule, which is still celebrated in the Shetland. In the past, barrels of burning tar were dragged through the village on sleds by guizers or men in strange costumes. A very rowdy event, it was consequently suppressed in Victorian times. The festival was altered somewhat when it was revived in the 19th century. Starting in 1889 a 30-feet-long (9 meters) Viking longship has been built each year. When the parade begins, the man elected as the Guizer Jarl, or master of ceremonies, stands on the ship with a band of men dressed as Vikings. The ship is pulled through the town followed by the pipers and other guizers in their wild costumes. At a designated location, the Vikings jump off the ship and it is burned. The guizers spend the rest of the night reveling.

WHUPPITY SCOURIE

The name of this festival is taken from a creature in a Scottish fairy tale, a story similar to that of Rumplestiltskin. The creature was a bad fairy who could only be defeated by someone who guessed her name.

In Lanark church bells are not rung during the winter months from October to February. Whuppity Scourie on March 1 marks the beginning of Spring when the bells are rung for the first time. At the first stroke of the bells, local children parade clockwise around the church, whirling paper balls around their heads. When the bells have finished ringing, the children compete to be the first to run three times around the church. Then the provost of the church throws a handful of coins and the children scramble to catch them.

Traditionally the ceremony was carried out by men, and they waved their hats over their heads. This hat waving often became rowdy and turned into fights, so the Victorians banned it. The essential ingredients of the festival—running clockwise round the church and whirling objects—probably dates back to a pagan ceremony to ward off evil spirits.

JEDBURGH BALL GAME

Jedburgh is one of the last remaining towns in Scotland to continue the tradition of ball games on Candlemas Day, which falls on February 2. According to tradition, the game was originally played with the severed heads of Englishmen. In modern times the balls are made of leather and stuffed with straw. Two teams of Uppies and Doonies—those who live north of the market square and those who live south—play out a vicious game of handball. The Uppies have to get the ball to their side of town, and the Doonies to theirs. At some stage the game ends on the frozen Jed River, and men commonly end up in the icy water.

Candlemas is the day in the Christian calendar when the baby Jesus was first presented at the temple. It marks the turning point in the year when the worst of winter is over. In Scotland there is an old saying "If Candlemas Day is fair and clear, there'll be two winters in one year." A fine February in Scotland is often followed by a harsh spring.

RIDING OF THE MARCHES

The Riding of the Marches is an ancient custom that was practiced in the border towns of Scotland during the Middle Ages. In some places it is a tradition that commemorates a local historical incident, most likely conflicts between the Scottish and English. The Riding, which involves gangs of young men galloping on horses around the town boundaries, is observed once a year at various times during the summer.

In Linlithgow 16 miles (26 km) west of Edinburgh, the ceremony is particularly spectacular with old-fashioned carriages and men dressed as heralds, halberdiers, and bailies—all ancient characters in the town's history. At Selkirk a standard bearer is chosen, and he parades through the town with a pipe and drum band. This is called "crying the burley," that is, calling all the riders to the ceremony. Banners of local regiments and craft guilds are then taken out of storage, decorated with flowers, and the parade begins. At the end of the Riding, the procession returns to town, and the flags are whirled around. In the afternoon there is a horse race.

The Ba' Game that takes place in the capital of Orkney on New Year's Day is similar to the Jedburgh ball game.

The Edinburgh Military Tattoo showcases military and civilian bagpipe bands, daredevil stunts, and traditional and contemporary music and dance performances. The Tattoo, meaning a performance of military music, takes place on the Edinburgh Castle esplanade.

THE EDINBURGH INTERNATIONAL FESTIVAL

The most famous of Scotland's modern festivals is the arts festival that takes place in Edinburgh in the fall. The Edinburgh International Festival is claimed to be the largest festival in the world. It first took place in 1947 and was organized by an Austrian, Rudolf Bing.

The festival was intended to be and still is a very highbrow affair with lots of performances of classical music and opera. In 1947 eight theater groups turned up uninvited and performed in church halls around the city. It was this unorganized element of the festival that gave rise to the Edinburgh Fringe Festival, one of the main attractions for people at the festival today.

The two events take place at the same time in late August, and over the years, hundreds of famous people have performed there; in some cases their Edinburgh show made them famous. Events range from operas to stand-up comedy, circus shows, and alternative theater as well as main stream performances and street theater. A jazz festival has been added as well as a television and film festival, and the Edinburgh Military Tattoo also takes place during the Festival.

About one-third of the tickets are bought by local people; the rest are bought by visitors from all around the world. Hotels and other accommodation fill up—every hall, school, and pub is used. On Festival Sunday a huge parade takes place in Holyrood Park in Edinburgh with fireworks and a concert in the evening.

OTHER FESTIVALS

Scotland has many other festivals. A number of them are held in summer, aimed partly at the scores of tourists who come to visit. In October there is the National Mod where Gaelic events including Highland dancing, Highland games, piping, and other performing arts are held. In September there are Highland games at Braemar as well as the Ben Nevis Race in which amateurs race to the top of Scotland's highest mountain. June sees the hockey finals at Inverness and the Royal Highland Agricultural Show in Edinburgh. In May there is another arts festival, this time in Glasgow, where a folk music festival is also held in July.

St. Andrew's Day (November 30) is a festival celebrated by expatriate Scots more than those who live in Scotland. Expatriate communities celebrate with pipe bands, *ceilidhs* ("KAY-lees"), meaning social gatherings, traditional food such as sheep's head and haggis, and whisky. In Scotland it is celebrated with a religious service in St. Andrews, where the saint's bones are kept.

The Edinburgh Fringe Festival has more than 500 theater companies giving thousands of performances at locations all around the capital.

FOOD

THE MENTION OF SCOTTISH FOOD immediately summons up images of haggis and oatmeal, which is strange since neither are originally or exclusively Scottish. Scottish cuisine was for many centuries centered on making use of every last scrap of food available. Lots of traditional Scottish dishes are based on this frugal attitude. In modern times Scots have developed a sweet tooth, and there are many puddings and cakes that are found only in Scotland. Immigrant communities have recently formed in the cities, and Indian and Chinese restaurants are the result of this cultural melting pot. In the 1980s and 1990s, increased wealth meant that people had more time for leisure activities and no longer regarded food as a matter of survival. In the cities restaurants serving cuisines from other parts of Europe and beyond have opened. In 1999, for the first time since records have been kept, the Scots spent more money on leisure activities, including eating in restaurants, than they did on their groceries.

Left: **Eating lunch in a cosy setting is something quite common for the Scots.**

Opposite: **A family having a Christmas dinner.**

Raw haggis at a shop window. When cooked, haggis is usually accompanied by mashed turnip and potato, and Scotch whisky.

HAGGIS

Haggis is a sheep's stomach filled with chopped organ meat, oatmeal, onions, and spices and simmered in a pot of water until cooked. It is traditionally served with bashed neeps (mashed turnip) and chappit tatties (mashed potato), and is especially popular on Burns Night, the anniversary of Robert Burns's birthday. Burns once wrote a poem dedicated to haggis, calling it "the Great Chieftain o' the Puddin' Race." There is even a vegetarian version of the haggis, although it is difficult to imagine how you could make one without using meat.

Every year a competition is held for the tastiest haggis, and butchers all over Scotland compete for the honor. Haggis is readily available in Scottish chippies, local fast food outlets, where it is served in a small sausage shape and deep fried. Until the 20th century, Haggis was as common in the rest of Britain as it is now in Scotland. It was only increasing wealth that drove the dish off English menus.

THE CHIPPIE

For generations in Scotland, as in the rest of Britain, most working people's idea of eating out was to head for the local chippie and buy bags of hot, deep-fried food, usually chips, which are like thick french fries. The usual accompaniment was deep-fried, battered fish, usually cod or haddock.

Chippies now sell sausage, haggis, burgers, and exotic options such as kebabs. One recent delicacy is deep-fried Mars bars. Mars bars, the chocolate and toffee bars that are Britain's most popular candy bar, are dipped in batter and deep fried. The sweet inside melts, while the batter holds the whole thing together. This unhealthy diet perhaps explains why Scotland has the highest rate of death from heart disease in Europe

In the past the food ordered by the customer was cooked on the spot, thrown in a greaseproof bag, covered in salt and vinegar, and wrapped in old newspapers to be carried home. After the European Union regulations were established, newspaper is no longer permissible, and styrofoam boxes and paper wrapping replace the older wrappings.

A big spread at a Scottish breakfast.

BREAKFAST

There are several types of Scottish breakfast foods to choose from. Least healthy but very popular with the Scots is the full Scottish breakfast, which consists of fried eggs, bacon, sausage, tomatoes, and occasionally white or black pudding, a kind of blood sausage. Another Scottish breakfast dish is Arbroath smokies, known in England as kippers. These were invented in Finnan, a village near Aberdeen, and are lightly smoked herring served with butter. Another alternative is smoked haddock served with a poached egg on top. Butteries, also known as Aberdeen rolls or rowies, are sometimes served as a second course after the hot dish. They are a specialty of the Aberdeen area, although they are sold all over Scotland. Unlike croissants, they are round and brown, but like croissants, they have a high butter content that makes them very soft and salty. They are served warm with butter.

Another breakfast choice in Scotland is oatcakes. Called breed in northeast Scotland, these are made with oatmeal and bacon fat. The ingredients are mixed into a dough with warm water and then cut into rounds, which are quickly fried on a griddle and then left to dry out. Scottish oatmeal or porridge comes in many forms, including instant microwaveable packets. Traditional porridge is made with pinhead oats, or oats that have not been crushed or rolled. The porridge takes about 45 minutes to cook and is served with salt and a side dish of cold milk. The oatmeal is spooned up and then dipped in the milk, and the little island of oatmeal sitting in a spoonful of milk is eaten. Scots never mix their oatmeal and milk together.

TRADITIONAL MAIN COURSES

Like the rest of Western Europe, the Scots have access to all the luxuries of the supermarket including instant meals and imported sauces and breads. A traditional Scottish evening meal might consist of Scotch broth, mince and tatties, cullen skink, clapshot, and stovies.

Scotch broth is a thick, wholesome soup made of various ingredients; the most important is barley, cooked with a mixture of either lamb or beef and vegetables. The dish takes some preparation because the barley and dried peas need at least 12 hours to soak before being cooked. The combined ingredients are cooked for two hours or more. In the old days the Scotch broth pot never left the stove; the last batch of broth forming the stock for a new pot of broth with a new set of ingredients.

Mince and tatties is similar to the English shepherd's pie. Minced beef, onions, and pinhead oatmeal are first fried and then mixed with some vegetables and braised in gravy. The dish is then served with boiled potatoes. Cullen skink is a soup made from smoked haddock, onions, and potatoes that originates in Cullen, a small town on the Moray Firth. It forms a thick, meaty stew rather than a thin soup and can be served with bread.

Stovies are a good way to use leftover, cooked meat. Potatoes and onions are cooked with gravy until tender and then the cooked meat is added along with seasonings. This is a very old dish with roots in the lives of the working poor, but it is often served at traditional *ceilidhs* or even weddings. It is usually served with oatcakes and a glass of milk. Clapshot is not a main dish but an accompaniment to meat dishes. It is a mixture of mashed potatoes, turnips, and onions.

In some areas, old-fashioned stoves such as this one are used. Instead of gas or electricity, peat is used to heat the stoves.

Above: **A popular Scottish biscuit is the shortbread. This butter cookie is often pie-wheeled shape.**

Right: **Scots pancakes can be eaten with syrup or butter and jam.**

SCOTTISH PUDDINGS

Scots like puddings, often the sweeter and stickier the better. As a rule most cakes in Britain are also found in Scotland but with the addition of a layer of confectioners sugar or granulated sugar. Scottish puddings include clootie dumpling, cranachan, and Scots pancakes. A particularly sweet dessert dish is Atholl brose.

Clootie dumpling is a mixture of fruitcake ingredients combined with lots of spices, molasses, and suet, all wrapped in a cloth and simmered in water for about four hours. This is served with custard or brandy butter and is similar in taste to the Christmas pudding served in Britain on Christmas Day. Any leftovers can be fried and served again.

Cranachan is the traditional harvest dish and is a very luxurious dessert. It is sometimes served at weddings. The table is laid with oatmeal, cream,

heather honey, whisky, and raspberries. The family sits down and serves themselves with whatever combination of these ingredients they love. Scots pancakes. They are made as a rich, creamy batter and then dropped a spoonful at a time on a hot griddle and cooked on both sides. They are served with Dundee preserves.

Atholl brose is similar to cranachan but is made with whipped cream, oats, and whisky and served in chilled dishes. The traditional New Year dessert is called black bun and is made from fruitcake baked inside a pastry case. Other Scottish sweet things are shortbreads made with lots of butter.

EATING OUT

The Scots have a good choice of places to eat, from authentic Indian and Chinese restaurants to Italian trattorias, pizza places, and brasserie-style cafés where a mix of traditional Scottish and innovative Californian styles predominate.

Fine dining is available in the larger cities. At the other end of the market the chippie is still going strong, and fish and chips is a popular choice. Fast food outlets fill the main shopping areas, and trendy café bars offer wine, coffee, and light meals.

Having a drink at a pub. Many pubs belong to breweries.

DRINKS

The most popular soft drink in Scotland is a fruit-flavored drink called Irn Bru. Tea is the next most commonly drunk beverage. It is drunk very hot and strong, with milk and sugar added. Beer is the next popular drink. Scotland makes several brands of beer. The more common lagers and blonde pilsner beers popular in North America and Europe are not so common here.

Beer in Scotland is measured in shillings—not its price in old English money but its alcoholic content. Most popular are heavy beers, which are about 80 shillings in strength (they actually cost about US$3.20 a pint). Beer is drunk by the glass (half pint) or by the pint, and heavy beer is a dark brown color with a white head of froth on it. It is often drunk in the form of a "nip and a haul," that is, served with a whisky chaser.

The national drink of Scotland is, of course, whisky, also known in Gaelic as the water of life. Whisky, which is one of Scotland's main exports, can be divided into two kinds. Single malt whisky, which is produced from only malted barley, and grain whisky, which is made from malted barley, unmalted barley, and maize.

Most whisky drunk in Scotland is a blend of grain and malt whisky, but the best is generally agreed to be single malt whisky, drunk without watering down to bring out the full flavor. Different distilleries produce different tasting whiskies depending on what peat, oak barrels, and peat source they use, and their tastes are very different.

RUMBLEDTHUMPS

Rumbledthumps is like clapshot and is made of potatoes, cabbage, onions, and cheese. The name for this dish means "mixed together."

1 lb ($\frac{1}{2}$ kg)potatoes, sliced thickly
1 lb ($\frac{1}{2}$ kg) white cabbage, spring cabbage, or kale, sliced
3 oz (114 g) butter
1 medium onion or the white part of two leeks, finely chopped
a little light cream
2 oz (76 g) sharp cheddar cheese, grated
fresh chives, chopped
pepper and salt to taste

Boil the potatoes in a little salted water. Once cooked, drain and mash. Simmer the cabbage gently in salted water. Melt the butter in a heavy-bottomed pan and cook the onions or leeks. Add the cooked potatoes and cabbage. Add the cream, season to taste, and beat together. Place the mixture in an ovenproof dish, cover with cheddar cheese, and grill or bake till brown.

Scottish records note that the earliest description of whisky making dates from 1494. Whisky grew in popularity after 1780 when a tax on wine made it unaffordable for most people. It was estimated that there were 8 licensed and 400 illegal stills in operation then. The government clamped down on illegal whisky distilling, driving many of the stills underground. In 1823 the production of whisky was legalized.

SCOTLAND

0   25   50 Miles

0   25   50 Kilometers

A   B   C   D

1

2

3

4

5

Legend:
- ● Capital city
- ● Major town
- ▲ Mountain peak

Feet	Meters
3,300	1,000
1,650	500
660	200
0	0

Unst

Shetland Islands

Lerwick

Orkney Islands

Hoy

Cape Wrath

Wick

Outer Hebrides

Lewis

St. Kilda

Harris

North Uist

Benbecula

South Uist

Sea of the Hebrides

Skye

Applecross

Culloden

Loch Ness

Moray Firth

Peterhead

Buchan Ness

Don

Inverurie

Aberdeen

Dee

Eriskay

Barra

Highlands

Cairngorms

Stonehaven

Great Glen

Ben Nevis
(4,406 ft/1,343 m) ▲

Grampian Mountains

Inner Hebrides

Mull

Iona

Loch Tay

Tay

Dundee

Arbroath

Perth

Firth of Tay

Comrie

St. Andrews

ATLANTIC

OCEAN

NORTH

SEA

Loch Lomond

Forth

Stirling

Central

Lowlands

Edinburgh

Firth of Forth

Kilmartin

Glasgow

Pentland Hills

Clyde

Lanark

Selkirk

Tweed

Biggar

Jedburgh

Southern

Uplands

Hawick

Firth of Clyde

Alloway

IRELAND

NORTHERN IRELAND

Gretna Green

Solway Firth

ENGLAND

Mull of Galloway

N

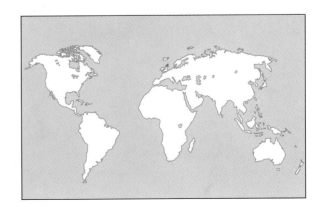

QUICK NOTES

OFFICIAL NAME
Scotland

AREA
30,418 square miles (78,783 square km)

POPULATION
5.2 million (1999 estimate)

CAPITAL
Edinburgh

MAJOR CITIES
Glasgow, Aberdeen, Dundee

RIVERS
Clyde, Forth, Tay, Tweed

LONGEST RIVER
Tay (117 miles/ 188 km)

ISLAND GROUPS
Inner Hebrides, Outer Hebrides, Orkney, Shetland

MOUNTAINS
Grampian Mountains

HIGHEST POINT
Ben Nevis (4,406 feet/ 1,343 m)

HIGHEST VILLAGE
Wanlockhead (1,380 feet/ 421 m)

CLIMATE
Temperate

LANGUAGES
English, Scots Gaelic, Scots

RELIGIONS
Church of Scotland, Free Church of Scotland, Roman Catholicism

CURRENCY
Pound sterling
US$1 = £0.6266 (2000)

MAJOR EXPORTS
Computers and electronics, fish and shellfish, oil and gas, whisky

MAJOR IMPORTS
Manufactured foodstuffs, machinery

MAJOR POLITICAL PARTIES
New Labour Party, Scottish Nationalist Party

NATIONAL FLAG
The cross of St. Andrew (Scotland's patron saint) set against a dark blue background

GLOSSARY

ceilidh ("KAY-lee")
A Gaelic word for "visit." It refers to a social gathering involving dancing, singing, storytelling, and drinking.

croft
Derived from the Gaelic *croit*, meaning a small area of land. Usually combines a house and land for cultivating or grazing.

dauphin ("DOH-phan")
The eldest son of the king of France.

firth
An indentation of the seacoast.

glen
A small, secluded valley.

guizers ("GUY-zers")
Participants of the Up-Helly-Aa, usually dressed in elaborate costumes.

haggis
A sausage made of chopped liver, heart and lungs of sheep, seasoned with spices, stuffed into a sheep's stomach and boiled.

Hogmanay
New Year's Eve.

kirk
A church.

lingua franca
Any language that is widely used as a means of communication among speakers of other languages.

pibroch ("PHIT-roch")
A series of mournful-like variations played on the Scottish Highland bagpipes.

sheriff
A county court judge.

sporran
A large purse, usually made of leather or fur, worn in front of a kilt on a belt.

taibhsearachd ("THAIBF-seer-a-chad")
Second sight.

tigh dubh ("TICHE DERBF")
Literally 'black house' and refers to the older type of croft houses.

Up-Helly-Aa
A fire festival held at Lerwick in the Shetland Islands, with its origins in an ancient Viking tradition.

BIBLIOGRAPHY

Cory, Kathleen B. *Tracing Your Scottish Ancestry*. Edinburgh: Polygon, 1996.

Dargie, Richard. *The Romans in Scotland*. Hove: Wayland, 1997.

Dargie, Richard. *Scotland in World War II*. Hove: Wayland, 1997.

Foley, Kathryn. *Victorian Scotland*. Hove: Wayland, 1997

Lerner Visual Geography: Scotland. New York: Sterling Publishing, 1973.

Paterson, Judy. *The History of Scotland for Children*. Broxburn: Glowworm Books, 1999.

INDEX

INDEX

INDEX

political parties:
Conservative, 29, 31, 39
Liberal Democrats, 34
New Labor, 33, 34, 38, 39
Scottish Labor, 30
Scottish Nationalist, 39
pope, 23, 24, 77
population, 7, 12–16, 27, 28, 30,
45, 51, 77, 87
Presbyterian, 25, 71, 73, 76
Protestant, 25, 101
publishing, 15, 16, 81
pubs, 60, 61, 66, 99, 110, 120
puddings, 113, 118

queens:
Anne, 26
Elizabeth I, 24
Elizabeth II, 34, 36
Mary Queen of Scots, 24, 102
Sophie of Hanover, 26
Victoria, 36

railroads, 15, 42, 44
rainfall, 10
raised beaches, 9, 19
Reformation, 24, 72, 73, 76, 83
restaurants, 113, 119
rivers:
Clyde, 8, 15, 21
Dee, 16
Don, 16
Forth, 8, 21
Jed, 108
Ness, 77
Tay, 8, 16
Tweed, 8
Rob Roy, 54, 92
Romans, 20, 21, 72

Sabbath, 75
salmon, 20, 45, 63, 102
sandstone, 9, 29
schools, 63, 64, 73, 75, 80, 81, 110
Scots, 21, 29, 52, 72, 80, 83
Scott, Sir Walter, 54, 56, 89, 92
Scottish Office, 33, 35
seas:
Atlantic, 7, 9
North, 7, 16, 17, 21, 31, 41, 43
Shakespeare, William, 22, 95
shipbuilding, 15, 16, 28, 30, 31, 41, 42

shortbread, 118, 119
skiing, 99, 103
soccer, 60, 99, 101
soccer clubs:
Glasgow Celtic, 101
Glasgow Rangers, 101
Manchester United, 101
Southern Uplands, 7, 8, 46, 51, 53
sports, 49, 59, 86, 99, 102
St. Columba, 72, 80, 85
St. Ninian, 72
Stone of Destiny, 23, 28, 29
superstition, 65, 71, 77
Sweden, 34, 55

taibhsearachd, 77
tanistry, 22
tartans, 26, 56, 57, 90
taxes, 25, 26, 33, 35, 39, 54, 121
tea, 120
television, 55, 59, 60, 81, 86, 89, 90,
92, 99, 110
tenements, 28, 96
theater, 60, 99, 110, 111
tigh dubh, 59, 62
tombs, 19, 69
tourism, 15, 41, 48, 49, 57, 69, 100, 111
towns:
Arbroath, 23, 29
Biggar, 106
Cullen, 117
Inverness, 111
Inverurie, 85
Jedburgh, 108
Lanark, 108
Lerwick, 107
Linlithgow, 109
Perth, 29
Peterhead, 45
Selkirk, 109
St. Andrews, 73, 102, 111
Stirling, 23
Stonehaven, 106
Wick, 106
trade, 26, 28, 30, 80
Trainspotting, 94
tweeds, 41, 48, 49

United Kingdom, 3, 30, 36, 41, 44
United Presbyterian Church, 75
United States, 27, 28, 30, 37, 48, 54,
55, 57

universities, 15, 55, 63

valleys, 9, 12, 15
Vikings, 21, 52, 79, 107
villages:
Alloway, 93
Braemar, 111
Comrie, 106
Finnan, 116
Gretna Green, 67, 68
Roslin, 75
Wanlockhead, 7
vowels, 81, 84, 85

Wales, 9, 33, 52, 59
Wallace, Sir William, 23, 94
weddings, 59, 67, 68, 117, 118
Westminster Abbey, 24, 29
whisky, 15, 41, 48, 105, 107, 111,
118, 120, 121
witchcraft, 71, 77
World War I, 30
World War II, 31, 41, 71, 77

PICTURE CREDITS
ANA Press Agency: 1, 9 (right), 40, 51,
59, 60, 79, 99, 111
Archive Photos: 24, 28, 50, 54, 55, 73,
92, 94
Camera Press Ltd: 37
Dave G. Houser: 26, 95, 116
Blaine Harrington: 48
Hutchison Library: 7, 9 (left), 16, 45, 49,
58, 62, 65, 72, 113, 120
International Photobank: 6, 10, 11, 14,
15, 19, 36, 57, 68, 71, 81, 93
Life File Photo Library: 106
Marshall Cavendish Picture Library: 13,
61, 74
North Wind Picture Archives: 20, 21,
25, 27, 52, 83, 85
Photobank Photolibrary Singapore: 4,
91, 102
David Simson: 53, 105, 107, 112, 115,
119
David Toase/Travel Ink: 78, 86, 110
Topham Picturepoint: 22, 29, 33, 34, 42,
44, 67, 69, 101
Trip Photographic Library: 3, 5, 12, 17,
18, 23, 30, 32, 38, 39, 41, 43, 46, 47,
63, 64, 66, 70, 76, 80, 87, 88, 89, 96,
97, 98, 100, 103, 104, 109, 114
(both), 117, 118, 123